One Way to God

Christian Philosophy and Presuppositional Apologetics Examine World Religions

Mike A. Robinson

Outskirts Press, Inc.
Denver, Colorado

The opinions expressed in this manuscript are solely the opinions of the author and do not represent the opinions or thoughts of the publisher. The author represents and warrants that s/he either owns or has the legal right to publish all material in this book.

One Way to God
Christian Philosophy and Presuppositional Apologetics Examine World Religions
All Rights Reserved.
Copyright © 2008 Mike A. Robinson
V2.0

Cover Photo © 2008 JupiterImages Corporation. All rights reserved - used with permission.

This book may not be reproduced, transmitted, or stored in whole or in part by any means, including graphic, electronic, or mechanical without the express written consent of the publisher except in the case of brief quotations embodied in critical articles and reviews.

Outskirts Press, Inc.
http://www.outskirtspress.com

ISBN: 978-1-4327-2295-1

Outskirts Press and the "OP" logo are trademarks belonging to Outskirts Press, Inc.

PRINTED IN THE UNITED STATES OF AMERICA

Contents

Dedication i

Introduction iii

Chapter 1 The One way to God 1
Chapter 2 Islam: The Religion of Allah 37
Chapter 3 Hinduism: The Religion of Karma 97
Chapter 4 Buddhism: The Religion of Buddha 135
Chapter 5 Increasing Discernment 173

Dedication

I offer this book to my dear Lord Jesus Christ, my Savior; mixed with error and sin, as are all my other deeds, which amount to nothing without His amazing grace. I dedicate this to world-wide minister, Nathan Ward and Gordon Smith; my brothers and friends, through whom God has blessed me in sundry ways; and who God sends to bless those ignorant of the true and living God: Go and preach the gospel, and "know nothing but Jesus Christ and Him crucified."

Introduction

THERE IS NO GOD BUT YAHWEH

> If you don't know where you are going, any road will take you there (Lewis Carroll).

A tale is told of a very artistic spider that built a beautiful and awe-inspiring web; it was a wonderful work of art. Many came to see its magnificence and symmetrical splendor. It was engineered with great precision and complexity. The little spider was glad that his work astonished so many. This motivated him to keep good and exact maintenance over it. Correspondingly, he would tighten a cord here and there, and then strengthen a string on the other side. One day, he noticed a large thread that didn't look useful. So, he cut it with his fangs, and as he bit through it, the whole web collapsed; and the little bug fell to the ground. The thread that he had just cut was the one essential thread that the whole web depended on. Once cut, it collapsed. Similarly, the Triune God is the grounding thread for a coherent web of beliefs (presuppositions). Those who reject Christian theism will tumble down into absurdity. The God of the Bible alone provides the foundation to attach a worldview that is both beautiful and enduring.

Necessary Preconditions

I will argue that Christianity alone provides the rational and moral necessities for intelligibility. That Christianity must be presupposed to make sense out of human experience. The non-Christian world religions deny Christian truth and leave the adherent into irrationality and condemnation. All men behave in rational and moral ways. However, only Christianity can account for the laws of reason and moral absolutes on which morality depends.

Here is the basis of my argument:

- Take p, which is a general principle or a law; and a universal or operational feature of human thinking or human experience.

- q (Christian worldview: which provides the necessary pre-essentials for the laws of logic and moral law) is the precondition of p (which requires the laws of logic and moral law).

- q is necessary to explain the possibility of p.

- q is presupposed by p; not merely deduced from p; not merely induced by p; nor merely analogous of p; but q is the presupposition of p.

- p is necessary for intelligibility.
- There is intelligibility.
- q is necessary.

Polytheism: Devoid of Ontological Necessities

> Therefore, since we have been justified through faith, we have peace with God through our Lord Jesus Christ (Romans 5:1).
>
> Because, indeed, because they have seduced My people, saying, "Peace!" when there is no peace (Ezekiel 13:10).
>
> May Mitra grant us peace!
> May Varuna grant us peace!
> May Aryama grant us peace!
> May Vishnu grant us peace!
> May Indra grant us peace!
> May Brishaspati grant us peace!
> (Self-stultifying poetry of the Hindu Upanishads)

The only ground for the necessary pre-essentials of the transcendent, atemporal, universal, and immutable laws of logic would have to be able to account for these pre-essentials by furnishing a ground, as Yahweh does, that is transcendent, atemporal, universal in knowledge, and immutable. A capricious monad god, Vishnu within polytheism or Poseidon within the college of gods do not offer these pre-essentials; and all the false deities fail to provide the rational and moral preconditions that Christianity delivers.

> What do I love when I love my God? Not the sweet harmony of song, not the fragrance of perfumes, not manna or honey, but when I love my God, I love a *certain* light (Augustine).

An epistemological ground that contains universals, changeless forms, and moral law cannot be overturned by appeals to experience. It deals with the required pre-environment to make experience intelligible. Since the laws of logic and fixed moral law are necessary to make experience intelligible, one cannot appeal to experience that is in constant flux to undermine them. Intelligible experience presupposes the laws of logic. Thus, A is A (Law of Identity) and A cannot be A and Non-A at the same time in the same manner (Law of Non-contradiction). What can supply the preconditions for these laws? Yahweh alone. No other deity has the attributes, the ontological essence, and epistemic credentials to supply these preconditions.

Universals and Immutables Furnished by Yahweh

If the laws of logic are conventional (true only because most men affirm them), then by definition they are not universals, therefore they are not true laws. Since one must employ the laws of logic as universals, one who attempts to deny their universality defeats himself. A God, who has universal power, position, and rule, as Yahweh does, alone provides the required preconditions for the universal laws of reason. This is an impregnable argument from a web of immutables, necessities, and universals that can only be unified and accounted for by Christian theism.

Anti-Yahwehistic religions must adopt positions that disallow certainty, necessity, and universality, but must surrender not just the laws of reason, but epistemology, ontology, ethics, and everything in human experience.

A god, among a pantheon of gods, is contingent and cannot produce universals, immutables, and necessities. For the lesser cannot provide the greater. Christian theism offers the rational man the only foundation for the possibility of making assertions, and even an assertion against Yahweh. Considering that the Triune God is the only possible epistemic ground, He is the lone source for universals and immutables that are utilized in all assertions. The ground necessary for assertions *must* supply non-material universals, unchanging things, and laws. Only the God of the Bible has these epistemological credentials.

Jesus' diagnosis of the world religions is severe.[1]

> I believe that all roads lead to the same place. We're taking different ways to get there, but we all end up in the same place. It's kind of like Kinky Friedman's statement, "May the God of your choice bless you" (singer Willie Nelson).

The Anti-theism of multitudinous religions (those that embrace a false deity) not only has inconsistent epistemological standards but also has self-rebutting standards. Some avow the notion that men observed golden plates, so they claim that one must base their religion on what can be seen or touched; this is a form of religious empiricism. In the spirit of that non-empirical concept (one cannot see or touch the idea of empiricism), the notion of empiricism cannot be the foundation for all knowledge. When the religious empiricist appeals to the observation by the five senses to define truth, he is dependent upon the immaterial laws of logic to make his definition; he must apply the laws of logic to observation. But he lacks the universal and necessary ground for these laws.

> Ned, have you thought about one of the other major religions? They're all pretty much the same (Lovejoy from *The Simpsons*).

The vital task of the thinking person is the task of criticism of falsehoods and rational inconsistencies. Many in the West believe that all religions are wacky myths or that they are all basically the same. This is *prima facie* not true and is self-refuting. Even the ultra-tolerant *Newsweek* magazine in 2007 admitted that "it is a fantasy to imagine that the world's two largest faiths (Christianity and Islam) are in any meaningful sense the same." Hindus, Newagers, Buddhists, and multifarious atheists believe that all religions are essentially alike; on the contrary, the religions disagree on almost every religious question. Christianity teaches that one is a sinner in need of a Savior and one is saved by grace through faith alone. Buddhists and Hindus believe that this world is an illusion. Buddhists focus on liberation from suffering and the self. Islam believes that the Trinity is false and that one must obey Allah to gain Paradise. Religion and anti-theism have fueled many wars and conflicts in history. Most multiculturalists deny that religions and cultures are dissimilar and incompatible. They insist that tolerance is the key to everyone "getting along." Some aspects and doctrines in diverse religions are similar. The entire field of world religions, but one (Christianity), profess that one has to work to merit his salvation or religious goals. It is believed to be possible through God's grace conjoined with the contribution of religionists. Christianity is the only religion that denies this proposition. The Christian faith alone contravenes the notion that salvation is grace plus works. One is saved by grace alone inasmuch as Jesus died on the cross for His people's sins and rose from the dead on the third day. All of the architects of various religions died and stayed in their graves, except for Christ. *Newsweek* added that it is a shibboleth that "all religions are the same."[2]

Significant Words, Terms, and Locutions

The following definitions are needed to provide clarity for the remainder of the book. If you are not familiar with apologetics and its terminology, you will want to put a bookmark on this page and refer to it until you are fluent with the vocabulary.

- **Apologetics:** The study and application of defending the faith. See 1 Peter 3:15; Jude 3; Acts 17-20.

- ***A Priori* Argument:** An argument prior to or independent of observation and experience, which is assumed to be true without the necessity to prove it. It is fully and universally independent of all experience, discernment, and discovery by the five senses.

- **Empiricism:** The belief that truth is to be found through the use of the five senses alone. Observation and measurement are the means to discover reality. Truth is discovered by the senses—what we can see, feel, observe, and measure.

- **Epistemology:** The study of how we know what we know; the nature and basis of knowledge; the accounting and justifying of knowledge claims; and the sources and scope of knowledge. Epistemic rights abide only in a system of knowledge that provides universals and invariants. "What do people ordinarily mean, when they say that they 'know' something?" (Greg L. Bahnsen: *Van Til's Apologetic*).

- **Immutable**: Unchanging; invariant; that which cannot change; always remaining the same; not mutable; changeless (God, the laws of logic, and moral law are immutable).

- **The Laws of Logic:** Abstract, non-concrete laws of thought and reason that are immaterial, universal, obligatory, necessary, and absolute. Some call them the laws of thought or the laws of reason. And a few scholars strongly prefer to name them as the laws of logic since they are independent of the minds of human beings. All rational communication and thinking assume the laws of logic. The most well-known law is the Law of Non-contradiction: A cannot be A and Not-A at the same time in the same way. A man cannot be his own father. The laws of logic reflect the nature and mind of God;

thus, they have ontological grounding—that is, they are grounded in the very nature of truth itself and cannot be reduced to human convention, opinion or psychology. Without these laws rational thinking is impossible. To deny the laws of logic, one must use these laws in attempting to deny them. Those who deny the laws of logic are participating in a self-refuting effort.

- **Presupposition:** Also known as First Principles. A preeminent belief held to be true and taken as a pre-commitment. It is the belief that is held at the most foundational level of one's grid or web of beliefs. It is the lens through which one interprets reality, taken for granted and assumed in making a statement or a theory. It is one's starting point; primary and fundamental assumption; and metaphysical foundation. Everyone has presuppositions—primary belief patterns that influence one's thinking and outlook. Reason, logic, and morality are only consistent with Christian presuppositions.

- **Rationalism:** The belief that truth is found only by the right use of reason and logic.

- **Transcendental Argumentation**: Bahnsen says, "A transcendental argument begins with any item of experience or belief whatsoever and proceeds, by critical analysis, to ask what conditions (or what other beliefs) would need to be true in order for that original experience or belief to make sense, be meaningful, or intelligible to us."

- **Universals**: Something that is true or applies everywhere and at all times. Immutable laws in mathematics and logic are universals.

- **Worldview**: An overall perspective of life. One sees and defines the world through his basic presuppositions, his worldview. It is the grid that one uses to evaluate reality.

- **Yahweh (YHVH/YHWH)**: The Lord God of the Bible sometimes called Jehovah and translated in the Old Testament as LORD (all caps). Christians profess that He is the Father, the Son, and the Holy Spirit as one God. He alone is the true and living God. He also calls Himself "I AM that I AM" (Exodus 3:14; John 8:24, 58). He is the only true and living God.

No God but God

> "You are My witnesses," says the LORD, "and My servant whom I have chosen, that you may know and believe Me, and understand that I am He. Before Me there was no God formed, nor shall there be after Me. I, even I, am the LORD, and besides Me there is no Savior" (Isaiah 43:10-11).

There are thousands of religions with a myriad and profusion of gods. But there is only one true God and that is the

God of the Bible. There is no God besides Him, considering that Yahweh alone provides the necessary rational, moral, universal, invariant, and uniform conditions for the intelligibility of the world.

> *The only way to avert skepticism is to have an unchanging, infinite, infallible, and exhaustive authority. The God of the Bible alone has these attributes. The Triune God is absolutely required because He is unchanging, universal in knowledge, timeless, transcendent, and immaterial; and the laws of logic are unchanging, universal, timeless, transcendent, and immaterial. The laws of logic are necessary for all assertions, investigations, ethics, and evidence; hence, God alone provides the necessary preconditions to make sense of our world and experience. The Triune God must exist, the contrary is impossible (My recapitulation of Van Til's and Bahnsen's basic argument which is the foundation for most of my apologetic claims).*

A changeless, omniscient, omnipotent rational ground and infrastructure is required to understand and account for our world. A young man roomed in a boarding house with a few folks including a retired music teacher. Every day, they had a little custom they both delighted in: the young man would come to the former music instructor's door and ask, "What's the good news today?" The teacher would grab his tuning fork, tap it on the side of his chair, and exclaim, "That's middle C! It was a middle C yesterday, it will be a middle C tomorrow; it will be a middle C ten-thousand years from now. The song writer upstairs sings flat, the guitar that Joe always strums is out of tune, but, my good boy, that is a middle C and it's fixed!" The music teacher rejoiced in the knowledge that there is a fixed constant that he could depend, an unchanging source that he could hold too. And it is good news that Yahweh is the necessary constant that is required for intelligibility of human experience.

Dependence on Previous Scholarship

I must state that this work is based on the brilliant apologetic system of Cornelius Van Til, Greg Bahnsen, and their disciples. The vast majority of the erudite theological and philosophical assertions and conclusions recorded in this book are to be accredited to their scholarship. Any faulty analysis, imprecise applications, and inaccuracies should be ascribed to me.

NOTES

1. William Edgar, *The Face of Truth*, (P & R, Phillipsburg: NJ, 2001), p. 121.
2. Newsweek, *True or False: The Major Religions Are Essentially Alike*, (New York: NY, July 2, 2007), p. 52.

CHAPTER One
There is One Way To God: The Certain Truth

Certainty is Certain

> Now I *know* that the LORD is greater than all the gods (Exodus 18:11).

> All flesh shall *know* that I, the LORD, am your Savior, and your Redeemer, the Mighty One of Jacob (Isaiah 49:26).

> That you may *know* and believe that the Father is in Me, and I in Him (John 10:38).

Above, I listed a few of the countless verses in God's word that reveal that one can know some things for certain. Job declared that he *"knows* his Redeemer lives." He was speaking with certain knowledge. The Triune God is the precondition for intellectual certainty. And certainty is a rational requisite. The stipulation that asserts that there is no certainty is self-rebutting, considering that it claims certainty: it asserts that it is certain that there is no certainty. Hence, there must be a certain, immutable, and infallible authority. The only one who can be that authority is God Almighty. All other philosophical launching points lack the ability to supply immutability and universality. Christianity is the inescapable truth inasmuch as it alone provides the preconditions for the universal and unchanging laws of logic. The Christian God alone is an immutable, transcendent, universal, and immaterial foundation; a plurality in unity. And the laws of logic are immutable, transcendent, universal, and nonmaterial; a plurality in unity. Human beings are not transcendent and immutable; thus humanity, without Yahweh, cannot account for the universals in the laws of logic, ethics, and mathematics. Universal and certain claims are inevasible, and Christianity alone provides the preconditions for universal and certain claims; thus, Christianity must be true and all other religions are false.

> Come near to Me, hear this: I have not spoken in secret from the beginning; from the time that it was, I was there. And now the Lord God and His Spirit have sent Me (Isaiah 48:16).

Without the Triune God (Father, Son, and Holy Spirit: One God), all reasoning is epistemically terminated; yet, there is reasoning and there must be reasoning. All non-Christian views of the creation come up epistemologically short and cannot make sense out of reasoning, science, and morality. A single person deity (Islam, Oneness Pentecostals, Jehovah Witnesses, and Sikhs) cannot account for the unity and diversity that subsists within the entire cosmos. Eastern religions cannot account for absolute morals and truth, as they hold the belief that everything is an illusion. Only the Christian world and life view can supply the necessary rational prerequisites for the immaterial, unchanging, and universal laws of logic. Consequently, it alone brings together the diversity within the unity of all things.

Rational Sight and Presuppositions

> Hearing you will hear and shall not understand, and seeing you will see and not perceive; for the hearts of this people have grown dull. Their ears are hard of hearing, and their eyes they have closed, lest they should see with their eyes and hear with their ears, lest they should understand with their hearts and turn, so that I should heal them. But blessed are your eyes for they see, and your ears for they hear (Matthew 13:14-16).

If a religionist or non-religionist comes to the knowledge game (epistemology or epistemic ground and rights), without depending on Christian presuppositions, he is epistemically blind. Christian presuppositions are the rational lenses that supply the immutables, universals, and immaterial necessities for making sense of human experience. When boxer Muhammad Ali fought Sonny Liston, he was winning in the early rounds through the use of his overwhelming speed and skills. Then Liston's cornerman put liniment on Liston's glove and in the next round it got into Ali's eyes and badly damaged his vision. Ali couldn't see and he had to fight blind. Liston won that round and would have won the match if Ali's sight remained blurred. Eventually it wore off and Ali could see again, and he won the fight. And the person, who views the world with non-Christian eyes, is blinded and cannot account for human experience. One needs, like Ali wiping off the liniment, sight to fight the rational fight.

Only the transcendent, aphysical, invariant, and multi-personal-unified God can provide the necessary preconditions for the transcendent, aphysical, invariant, and multi-unified laws of logic. I will argue from the shoulders of giants as I press the truth that there is "absolutely certain proof for the existence of God and the truth of Christian theism. Even non-Christians presuppose its truth while they verbally reject it."[1] We ask the nonbeliever "what are the conditions that make thought possible?"[2] Only the Triune God can furnish those preconditions to establish the rational flooring for intelligibility. I will attempt to refute non-Christian religions with what Van Til called "the method of implication into the truth of God a transcendental method. That is, we must seek to determine what presuppositions are necessary to any object of knowledge in order that it may be intelligible to us."[3]

Have No Other Gods

> And God spoke all these words, saying: "I am the LORD your God, who brought you out of the land of Egypt, out of the house of bondage. You shall have no other gods before Me. You shall not make for yourself a carved image, or any likeness of anything

that is in heaven above, or that is in the earth beneath, or that is in the water under the earth; you shall not bow down to them nor serve them. For I, the LORD your God, am a jealous God, visiting the iniquity of the fathers on the children to the third and fourth generations of those who hate Me" (Exodus 20:1-5).

The Ten Commandments are in the news frequently in the United States. Many American citizens want to see them displayed in the courthouse and the school house, yet simultaneously they insist that they are secular and all Americans can uphold them. They claim that all people, of all faiths, can affirm them. Yet the reality is that the Buddhist, the Hindu, and the Muslim, among many other groups, do not believe in the first three commandments. Yahweh is God, and the first three commandments demand full allegiance and worship be given to Him alone. The other seven commandments reflect His nature and are eternally linked with the first three commandments of the Decalogue.

John Calvin avouched in his sermon on Galatians that "the Law...serves also for our instruction, that we might learn to discern between good and evil, and again it quickens us up, as though God should give us strokes with the spur, to make us apply ourselves the more diligently unto him." The law is for instruction in the manner in which one must serve God first and humanity second. It never crossed Luther's mind that the commandments were secular for he preached that the law is "a kind of bridle by which [people] are kept in the fear of God." He added: "Anyone who knows the Ten Commandments perfectly knows the entire

Scriptures." One reason that the Ten Commandments are weighty and consequential is that they call men to worship only the true and living God.

The Westminster Shorter Catechism instructs us on the application of the first commandment:

> Question 46. What is required in the first commandment?
> Answer. The first commandment requires us to know and acknowledge God to be the only true God, and our God; and to worship and glorify him accordingly.

The Flying Spaghetti Monster and All False gods Fail to Provide Intelligibility

The God of the Bible is the One and only. There are no other gods in existence, except in the emotional idol factories of men. Thus, God has the authority to require all men, in all ages to honor Him alone. The first commandment bans people, without exception, from worshipping all false gods, whether that is Thor, Ra, Ram, Baal, Krishna, the Flying Spaghetti Monster, Dagon, Shiva, Brahma or any other false god. The literal injunction is to have no other gods before God's face. God sees everything. And He mandates that all men dispel other deities from their heart, life, and worship. All claims from other gods are just the notions of men void of true revelation. The first commandment is the most sacred of all the commandments: we are bound to affirm and profess that there is but one God only; the Most High, and to honor and worship Him alone.

Please note: I employ the word "God" only in reference to the one true and living Triune God: the Father, and the Son, and the Holy Spirit: one God. No other false deities or gods are referenced in my usage of the capitalized word "God" in English.

Do Not Take the Lord's Name in Vain

Our duty is to uphold God's honor and His name. This forbids people to replace God's name with the name of a pagan deity. The statute which forbids the taking of the Lord's name in vain requires mankind to respect and honor His holy name, to not profane His being or name. The word "vain" means uselessness, vanity, emptiness or nothingness. The imperative is to never blaspheme, utter, declare, speak or use God's name in a disrespectful, idle or a deficient fashion. Our obligation is to respect God's name and to never treat it lightly. We should regard His name as holy and revere it because there is only one true and living God, all the other gods are false gods and they do not exist.

> The third commandment requires the holy and reverent use of God's names, titles, attributes, ordinances, word, and works. The third commandment forbids all profaning or abusing of anything whereby God makes himself known (Westminster Shorter Catechism: Answers 54-55).

Presuppositions

Everyone has presuppositions. All atheists, religious people, and Christians have presuppositions. Presuppositions are the intellectual goggles through which we interpret the world, the basic assumptions we take for granted. These foundational pre-inferences are the preconceived notions that are rarely challenged; all men have them. Presuppositions drive what you believe and the way you view life, and most people are unaware of them. Allotheists have their foundational assumptions about life and the world. They live most of their lives employing basic principles that are inconsistent with their worldview. Much of how they live is consistent with the Christian worldview; they take their presuppositions for granted and rarely scrutinize them or follow them to their analytical conclusion. All of us should be aware of our assumed biases. We should acknowledge the rational inclinations that we all bring to the quest for knowledge. All religionists ought to be tough-minded and examine basic beliefs.

Presuppositions often operate like personal tastes, as when you walk into a candy store. As your eyes run across the shelves, without even thinking, you automatically, by custom and taste, eliminate what type of candy you do not enjoy. You do not even mark in your mind, say, the dark chocolate. You move on to that which is pleasant for your personal taste and you choose from that section of goodies. Your tastes and preferences have acted as "a screen," as a type of presupposition. And in theology, philosophy, and intellectual growth, one must interpret within their own conceptual web. All thinking people have presuppositions. Islamic terrorists have the presupposition that they should attack anyone who disagrees with Islam. Buddhists believe that all is an illusion, so they do not care about avoiding hell.

A "presupposition" is an elementary assumption in one's reasoning or in the process by which opinions are formed. As used here, a "presupposition" refers not to just any assumption in an argument, but to a personal commitment, which is at the most basic level of one's network of beliefs. Presuppositions form a wide-ranging, foundational perspective (or starting point) in terms of which everything else is interpreted and evaluated. As such, presuppositions have the greatest authority in one's thinking, being treated as your least negotiable belief and being granted the highest immunity to revision.[4]

Bahnsen further notes that "Christian epistemology (or theory of knowledge), in contrast to non-Christian religions, should thus be elaborated and worked out in a way that is consistent with its own fundamental principles (or presuppositions), lest it be incoherent and ineffective. It has been Van Til's aim to bring this ideal of 'epistemological self-consciousness' to bear upon the theory and practice of defending the Christian faith." The non-Christian worldview is self-contradictory and we demonstrate this as we "reason from the impossibility of the contrary."[5] Van Til's slogan: "Anti-theism presupposes theism" also includes the non-Christian religions of the world. Islamic, Buddhist, Hindu, and all false religions, according to the Bible, are anti-theistic. Van Til demonstrated that "a transcendental analysis...would show that the possibility of its coherence or meaningfulness assumes the existence of God that it denies."[6] The devout and the nonobservant peoples of all non-Christian religions are bound to the same laws and universals that Christians are tied to. Still, only Christianity can theologically and philosophically tender the ground for these laws.

Reason Grounded on Yahweh

Not only do many religionists despise reasoning but they also cannot even account for reason. They can be reasonable, but cannot explain where reason comes from or why one should be reasonable. They cannot account for or justify human reason. Eastern religionists, if asked why reason is useful, may say, "It's an illusion, one is not bound to Western logic." What is striking is that denial of the laws of logic is stuck utilizing the laws of logic. Thus, the non-Christian has self-defeating faith.

Logic is a Christian Actuality

> In the beginning was the Logos, and the Logos was with God, and the Logos was God (John 1:1).
>
> The eternal Logos is a necessary condition...of human knowledge about anything.[7]

Jesus' ontology (His being and essence) is a substantial element of Christianity, for He is the great Logos (John 1:1), and logic is an element of His being and nature. Christians are the only community that can account for reason; as reason comes from the nature of God. The true God is the God of reason. Reason cannot be held over His head in a type of Eurythro Dilemma, but is a reflection of His nature; and we must espouse it in submission to His revelation in the Bible. Christians should base their worldview on God's word and His character. Logic has no physical content. One cannot put it in a bowl and pour milk over it. The abstract application of reason also has no material content.

The laws of logic are essential and a precondition for any communication. Logic is the foundational instrument necessary for all utterance, debate, science, mathematics, and learning. Without using the laws of logic, one could not deny that logic is mandatory for communication. The precondition for the laws of logic is the God of the Bible. Without the transcendent and universal God Almighty, one could not justify or account for the transcendent and universal rules of logic. Yahweh is the precondition for laws of reason. The laws of thought are the precondition for knowledge, discourse, and argument. Logic is absolutely necessary for the intelligibility of life and God is absolutely necessary for logic. Thus, the Triune God is, and has to be. And He alone is God. No other named god supplies the obligatory preconditions for the intelligibility of this world.

The Way to Find the Truth

> For thus says the LORD, Who created the heavens, Who is God, Who formed the earth and made it, Who has established it. ... Who formed it to be inhabited: "I am the LORD, and there is no other. I have not spoken in secret. ... I, the LORD, speak righteousness, I declare things that are right. ... They have no knowledge, who carry the wood of their carved image, and pray to a god that cannot save. Tell and bring forth your case; yes, let them take counsel together. Who has declared this from ancient time? Who has told it from that time? Have not I, the LORD? And there is no other God besides Me, a just God and a Savior; there is none besides Me.

> Look to Me, and be saved, all you ends of the earth! For I am God, and there is no other" (Isaiah 48:18-22).
>
> The question of world religions has its answer here (in Jesus). There is an exit, which is at the same time the entrance to life. It is through Jesus Christ—the way, the truth, and the life.8

My wife took my i-pod off our dinning table and put it on an obscure shelf before she ate lunch. When I returned home and found it missing on the table, I phoned my wife. She said that she needed space to eat and so she put my iPod away. I asked her how I could find my iPod now that she moved it to an unknown location. She told me that she had put a post-it note on the iPod. That, of course, would not have done me, her befuddled husband any good. The portable stereo would have been hidden, and a note on a hidden stereo was lost to me until my wife informed me where she put it. Such is the problem of an unsaved person. He is lost, and cannot use his own reason or experience to find his way to truth. He is lost, and his autonomous reason is lost with him. The only way he can find the truth is through an objective, unchanging source. The God of the Bible is the unchanging rational bedrock and fountainhead.

The biblical God is the pre-necessity for self-knowledge and the intelligibility of the world. Without God, man is lost, holding his own note of a man-made holy book. Only through Yahweh and His revelation can a man be found and have an objective basis for truth. God is the absolute and transcendental necessity for the intelligibility of all human apprehension. He is the precondition for the grounding and understanding of knowledge. Buddhism, Hinduism, and atheism cannot justify knowledge or truth. If you do not presuppose the truth of God in Christ, you cannot make sense out of the cosmos and all of reality. Christianity is true not because it makes better sense, but because it alone supplies the foundation for logic; it is true because without it you cannot make sense of anything. All other religions, philosophies, and worldviews lack the transcendentally required precondition (Yahweh) for intelligibility, logic, ethics, and truth.

> Jesus said to him, "I am the way, the truth, and the life. No one comes to the Father except through Me" (John 14:6).

There is Mountainous Evidence and Documentation for Scripture

The Bible supplies a massive pile of *a posteriori* evidence. It reveals to humanity that the Earth hangs on nothing (Job 26:7) and is a sphere (Isaiah 40:22). Scripture declared these observable and testable facts thousands of years before telescopes and modern science discovered them. God's word declared to humanity the proper function of the water cycle (Job 38:12-14), the existence of ocean currents (Psalms 8:8), the solar cycle, and the expansion of the universe (Isaiah 40:22) centuries before modern science discovered these verifiable truths. These facts are accordant with the Bible. They, and other evidence, do not give the Bible authority; it is crowned with it because it is God's word. All science, testing, and analysis presuppose biblical revelation. Testing utilizes a number of disciplines, such as the laws of reason and induction. We have sure knowledge that the God of Scripture lives. We do not think He *probably* exists; our faith is not just *reasonable* or *plausible*. It is impossible for the true and living God *not* to exist, because without Him we can know nothing at all. He is the precondition for all knowledge. Yahweh must be pre-assumed as the basis of every element of mankind's experience.

Yahweh is the Fount and Foundation for All Reality

Consider the following syllogism:

- Yahweh is the foundation of all reality; or, reality is unintelligible.
- Reality is intelligible.
- Therefore, Yahweh is the foundation of reality.

The consequence of asserting that Yahweh is not the only God is that the world becomes unintelligible and absurd. But the proposition of God's refutation is impossible because it is self-immolating. Van Til captured this when he wrote that the non-Christian, in his "negation of God, is still really presupposing God." He adds that "anti-theistic knowledge is self-contradictory on its own ground, and that its conception of contradiction even presupposes the truth of Christian theism."[9] If the world is unintelligible and unknowable, then that statement itself would be unintelligible and unknowable; and hence self-voiding and fallacious. Accordingly, Yahweh must be the ground and foundation of knowledge. Unless Christianity is true, we can know nothing of reality. If we can know nothing of reality, we cannot know even the proposition that we know nothing. Unless the God of revelation is and has spoken, human knowledge has no intelligible basis. God's word declares that life must revolve around Him. We must have no other gods before Him.

The Anti-theists

Some allotheists state that belief in the incarnation of Jesus Christ is unjustified and lacking in evidence. This statement lacks evidence; and is more than problematic. Non-Christian religions cannot even account for the reality of evidence or the discovery of apparent problems. They must stand on the Christian worldview to discuss evidence and problems. Only Christianity can have a justified basis for the evaluation of evidence and the intelligent identification of problems. Those who deny the incarnation of Christ assert that which is unintelligible, because the assertion disqualifies itself, since Christianity accounts for intelligibility and non-Christian thought cannot. Thus, non-Christian thought is self-defeating, like all systems that reject God's word.

God Completes All That He Begins

> Thus says the LORD, the King of Israel, and his Redeemer, the LORD of hosts: "I have declared the former things from the beginning; they went forth from My mouth, and I caused them to hear it. Suddenly, I did them, and they came to pass. ... And now the Lord GOD and His Spirit have sent Me. Thus says the LORD, your Redeemer, the Holy One of Israel: I am the LORD your God" (Isaiah 44:6-8; 48:3-20).

Another area of evidential attestation for Christian theism is the Messianic prophecies fulfilled by Jesus Christ. The Old Testament prognosticated the coming of the Messiah in exact detail. The text, written centuries before the coming of Jesus, prophesied over three hundred facts about Him. No other originator of any religion can provide a similar record of his life written centuries before his birth. Religious founders like Joseph Smith, Mary Baker Eddy, David Koresh, Muhammad, and Buddha cannot supply a widely transmitted, preexisting record that accurately stated in advance the details of their lives. The three hundred clear prophecies of the coming Messiah were ordained by God. The Lord revealed historical facts about the coming of Jesus prior to His birth. All these prophecies came to pass in the birth, life, death, and resurrection of Jesus of Nazareth.

Christ's virgin birth was foretold about seven hundred years before He was born: "So, the Lord Himself shall give you a sign. Behold, the virgin will conceive and shall bring forth a son, and they shall call His name Emmanuel" (Isaiah 7:14). His place of birth was foretold: "And you, Bethlehem...out of you He shall come forth to Me, to become Ruler in Israel, He whose goings forth have been...from eternity" (Micah 5:2). The precise date of His entry in Jerusalem was forecast in the book of Daniel.

The event of Christ's death on the cross was recorded prior to His advent. The documentation of this event preceded the actual historical incident before that manner of execution was even invented, notably in Isaiah and the Psalms. Psalms 22:15-16 announced the crucifixion several centuries before it happened: "For dogs have circled around me; the band of spoilers have hemmed me in, they pierced my hands and my feet." This documentation is astounding. The truth is even more certain and compelling than great blocks of evidence one might compile to prove the facts of Christianity. The argument for Jesus Christ is certain. Only the biblical God can provide the necessary preconditions for factualness and certainty.

The Triune God Exists Necessarily: The Argument

> God is in heaven; He does whatever He pleases (Psalms 115:3).

A simple argument is: Without the Triune God one cannot account for anything: including personal identity, communication, love, unity, coherence, fixed ethics, predication, deduction, reasoning, and more. The Lord God of the Bible is the precondition for the laws of logic, invariants, morality, mathematics, and everything else in the cosmos. These universals are necessary for understanding human experience. Only Yahweh can account for universals and rational necessities. Hence, Christian theism is certain and ineludible.

> When you lift up the Son of Man, then you will *know* that I am He (John 8:28).

One must be certain of something, because to assert that no one can know anything for certain would require one to be certain of that proposition. There has to be certainty in our world to know anything. And we must know something, or again we fall into self-contradiction. The problem is that, to truly know anything, one must either have all knowledge or hear from one who does. Only an omniscient being can be the epistemic bedrock for universals and absolutes. No finite man could know universals unless an omniscient and infinite being revealed it to him. And God has revealed truth and the laws of thought to man; therefore, we can have knowledge. Without the God of Abraham, Isaac, and Jacob one can have no knowledge; that is a self-refuting proposition because it is a knowledge claim. Thus, it is necessary and certain that the true God must live.

Mundane aspects of life demonstrate that we must have prior rational pre-commitments to make any affirmation. We are rationally obligated to presuppose many laws, forms, and norms in order to disseminate thoughts with others. All those necessary presuppositions make dialogue possible. Thus, without presupposing the existence of the tri-personal God of the Bible, one cannot account for communication. Language, predication, and communication would be impossible without God. Only Christianity has a relational God, who supplies rational epistemic guarantees.

> The glory of Christ in His exaltation lies in the infinite love that God the Father has for Him.[10]

The Multitudinal Evidence for the God of the Bible

> He also presented Himself alive after His suffering by many infallible proofs, being seen by them during forty days and speaking of the things pertaining to the kingdom of God (Acts 1:3).
> "Present your case," says the LORD; "bring forth your strong reasons, says the King of

Jacob. Let them bring forth and show us what will happen; let them show the former things, what they were, that we may consider them, and know the latter end of them; or declare to us things to come. Show the things that are to come hereafter, that we may know that you are gods" (Isaiah 41:21-23).

There is ponderous evidence that the God of the Bible exists, but the evidence alone will not convert a non-Christian into a Christian. The bare facts of the more than three hundred Messianic prophecies are astounding and convincing to me as a Christian. I love the evidence that God has given us. The prophecies that foretold the birth, life, and death of Jesus are found in Genesis 3:15, 49:10; Psalms 2:6-7; Psalms 22; Micah 5:2; Daniel 9:25; Zechariah 9:9, 12:10; Isaiah 7:14, 9:6, 53; and many other passages. These prophecies are recorded in the Dead Sea Scrolls and the ancient Jewish Targums (translations of the Old Testament distributed before Christ) and were written before the birth of Christ; and every one of them was fulfilled by Jesus.

Scholar Peter Stoner calculated the odds as 10^{157} that merely forty-eight of these predictions could be fulfilled by chance. The Theory of Probability declares that odds greater than 10^{50} are the same as zero; and 10^{157} is much larger than that. Hence, the life of Jesus was ordained by God Almighty. The Messianic prophecies are unique and stunning. The accuracy and specific detail of the events that the Bible prophesied are astonishing. They are not vague generalities; the Messianic prophecies are unblenched, startling, detailed, precise, and all point to Jesus Christ.

> All things must be fulfilled, which were written in the Law of Moses, the Prophets, and the Psalms concerning Me (Jesus, Luke 24:44).

Christianity alone has a risen Savior. The historical and biblical testimony concerning the resurrection of Jesus Christ is convincing to me and other believers as well. Those outside the true faith have a different set of presuppositions, which complicates the communication of the evidence. The Scriptures do not instruct us to press the *prima facie* evidence, but to profess the *a priori* necessity of the truth of Christianity. The God does not *probably* exist. The argument from the impossibility of the contrary demonstrates that the God *must* exist. The God of the Bible is the precondition for all argument, proof, evidence, and reason. It is impossible for God not to exist, inasmuch as He is the precondition for all intelligent exchanges. The aphysical, universal, and unchanging God alone provides the necessary preconditions for the use of aphysical, universal, invariant laws of logic. To argue at all, one must presuppose that God lives. It is impossible for Jesus not to be Lord of all. No other deity can fill this necessary role.

The true God is the only Precondition for Intelligibility

The converse of Christianity, religious or anti-religious, is impossible inasmuch as all other worldviews fall into absurdity, self-contradiction, and conclusions contradictory to their own assumptions. An important part of life is to ask questions. The primary question one must ask is: What will supply the preconditions to make reality intelligible? Without God, nothing comports with reality, and nothing can make sense; that is the biblical truth. The true and living God is the precondition for the intelligibility of reality, and the understanding of all human experiences. The truth from the word of God will dislodge unbelievers from their self-deceptions and delusions because of the self-defeating nature of their intellectual pre-commitments.

The Evidence is Astonishing

Evidence is indeed wonderful. Unlike other religious systems, the Christian faith has a lot of evidence to support its claims. In truth, there is nothing *but* evidence for the God of the Bible. Every planet and every pebble declare the splendor and power of Yahweh (Psalms 19:1). We see the evidence of God's fingerprints in every corner of the universe. Mankind discovers the proof and affirms the facts that the Bible records and announces. The greatest miracle is the resurrection of Jesus. Jesus is alive, He is risen from the grave. He is the only religious leader in history to rise from the dead. He is the only one who pre-announced a resurrection, and He engineered and carried out His promise. You can sojourn to the tombs of the religious leaders, who have succumbed to the grim reaper, and find their remains still in the grave. You can visit their occupied graves just as you can those of heterodox leaders like David Berg, Mary Baker Eddy, Brigham Young, and Muhammad. They and all the others died and stayed dead; their occupied tombs attest to it. Jesus Christ, however, is alive through His resurrection. His sepulcher is vacant.

Jesus Christ heralded, "All power on Earth and heaven has

been given to me" (Matthew 28:18). No power could have kept Him in the tomb. The Romans killed Him, put Him in a grotto tomb, and placed colossal stone at a downgrade angle in front of the cave, attached Caesar's seal on the grave cave, and posted Roman guards to protect the sepulcher. They were only trying to prevent the inevitable. Jesus had the authority and power to ascend out of the tomb, and nothing could stop Him. God used Christ's resurrection and appearance before His disciples, and He used the subsequent preaching of the Apostles, to win many of Christ's enemies to salvation. Luke informs us that "the word of God spread, and the number of the disciples multiplied greatly in Jerusalem; and a great many of the priests were obedient to the faith" (Acts 6:7).

Men do not go to their death willingly if they *know* they have been deceived. Islamic suicide bombers die, believing in the notion that they will go to Paradise after murdering people for Islam. They do not base their actions on a belief in an eyewitness report, but on their feelings. If they were to blow themselves up as an act of faith in believing that hundreds of people had observed their Ayatollah die and rise from the dead, that would be analogous to Christianity. But the Islamic *martyrs* die without affirming a historical fact that would rationally vindicate their faith. The followers of Jesus died for Him on the basis of seeing, holding, and hearing the risen Jesus. So many die for lies, but not for what they know is a lie. The followers of David Koresh—the people who knew that he was a fraud—tried to escape the Branch Davidian compound before and during the government siege. Once they knew that Koresh was a Messianic impostor, they ran and jumped to safety. Many others tried to escape and were shot.

The only God of Love

> Love...rejoices in the truth; bears all things, believes all things, hopes all things, endures all things. Love never fails (1 Corinthians 13:4-8).
>
> God is love (1 John 4:8).

The non-Christian cannot account for or posit certain justification for anything. They cannot tell the versant believer, under the scrutiny of inquiry, where anything comes from or why one should affirm any thought or proposition. Only the Christian conceptual scheme can account for ethics, identity, motion, necessity, induction, and even love. Ask the Muslim, "What is love?" The Koran never declares that Allah is love. Hinduism and Buddhism teach that everything is an illusion. That would include love. But all men know that love is real and that it is not an illusion. The one and true God is the Father, Son, and Holy Spirit. Love exists because God is "supremely personal. ... He is a communion of three persons."[11] God is three eternal persons loving one another infinitely and perfectly.

> The sum of all God's love is His love to Himself.[12]

Throughout eternity, the heavenly Father loved the Son and the Holy Spirit. The Spirit loved the Father and the Son, as the Son also loved the Father and the Spirit. Only the one eternal God in three persons can reveal where love came from and what love is. No other religion can justify or ultimately explain love, because their gods do not coexist in one being as infinite, immutable, and loving persons. The

Father, Son, and Holy Spirit have eternal, unchanging love among the Godhead. Yahweh alone is God, and He alone can be the eternal ground for love. The love and the fellowship among the persons in the Godhead are the pattern and the source of human love and interpersonal communication. We love others because we bear the image of God. There are three persons in the Godhead—the Father, the Son, and the Holy Spirit—and these three are one God, Yahweh, the same in substance, and equal in power and glory.

Christianity Accounts and Grounds Eternal Love

One of the best ways to expose the self-deception of the allotheist is to play a little coy and pose questions. The topic of love is a wondrous thing to explore with non-Christians. It is worth noting that of the 99 attributes of for Allah, not one is love. The Mormon god progressed to godhood; thus, he was not always god; and hence, he could not be the source of eternal love. Eastern religions claim that reality is a mere illusion; therefore, love must be an illusion. The atheist has no ultimate answers in regard to love. Only Christianity can account for love. Love comes to us through the Triune God. God's nature is the ultimate and objective basis of love. Real love is objective and eternal because it is an eternal attribute of the eternal God. God presupposes love, and love presupposes God. Christians can justify love, and we should share that love.

The Only True and Living God: Father, Son, and Holy Spirit

"You are My witnesses," says the LORD, "and My servant whom I have chosen; that you may know and believe Me, and understand that I am He. Before Me there was no God formed, nor shall there be after Me. I, even I, am the LORD, and besides Me there is no Savior" (Isaiah 43:10-11).

Only Christianity presents the only true God as the Father, the Son, and the Holy Spirit: one God in three persons. There is no other God in whom we must believe. He is the only God who lives, and the only God who is necessary.

Nonexistent Deities Cannot Help

The false gods of non-Christian religions cannot assist or deliver anyone. These gods do not exist, for they are made in the image of man. The only God, whose existence is not contingent on men, is the God of the Bible. The Mormon gods, the Hindu gods, and the Sikh god do not have necessary existence. There are worlds in which these gods would not exist. They are not necessary in all possible worlds. They are not logically and ontologically necessary beings. Only the Triune God of Scripture is the precondition for the intelligibility of this world, and any realm, dimension or world one could imagine. He is necessary, not contingent. The entire cosmos is reliant upon God. Yahweh is necessary; it would be impossible for the Lord God not to exist. The Almighty is all-sufficient, all-knowing, and all-powerful in His sovereignty. God is not dependent on anything in any world. The world is completely dependent on Him. All existence, all opinions, and all debate presuppose the God of Jacob.

The Christian Alone Has True Certainty

> These things I have written to you who believe in the name of the Son of God, that you may *know* that you have eternal life, and that you may continue to believe in the name of the Son of God (1 John 5:13).

The Lord God does exist, and we can have complete certainty of His sovereign being. Paul declares that he knows in whom he has believed (2 Timothy 1:12). It is impossible for the Christian worldview to be false. The intelligibility of human experience requires the God of the Bible. Christianity is the only worldview that provides human reason an unchanging foundation for knowledge. All non-Christian religions and systems of thought fail to furnish a foundation for the Law of Non-contradiction. Thus, they cannot provide the footing for knowledge and can offer only an antithetical and incongruous worldview. Unless you believe in God's revealed word in the Bible, you cannot account for anything in the universe. God is the underlying and infinite ground for all knowledge, proof, evidence, and logic. It is impossible for God not to exist. He is the precondition for all knowledge since knowledge requires the use of the rules of logic. The omniscient, nonmaterial, and unchanging Yahweh alone provides the necessary preconditions for the use of nonmaterial, universal, and unchanging laws of logic. To argue at all, you must presuppose that the true God lives; you must use logic. Anti-theistic thought cannot supply the necessary preconditions for the laws of logic; thus, they fall into futility because of the internal contradictions in which they are entangled. Thus, the contrary of Christianity is impossible, absurd, and self-rebutting on its own assumptions. Without the Triune God, there could not be knowledge, and nothing could make sense; and that is self-refuting, and hence impossible.

God: One that Men would not Make Up

Yahweh is not a God that one would make up if left to himself. Christian theology declares a revelation from a source that transcends mankind. Christians must proclaim that God is the Father, and the Son, and the Holy Spirit; one God, unique, and indivisible; alone in majesty, clothed in splendor, might, and holiness. The Triune God reveals so much of His nature that is awesome and frightening, righteous and unbending. So much of the sovereign God is mysterious and overwhelming. Even some Christians attempt to apologize for God's attributes, and many professed believers are unwilling to follow Him. They want to make Him more "kinder and gentler." They attempt to do a little tinkering with His character, so that God comes across nicer and less holy. We must resist this compromise. God is majestic and awesome, and He is Almighty.

The Father, Son, and Holy Spirit: One God is Necessary

A unitarian god is fallacious and one can discover this just by a quick perusal of the literature of the religions of the singular-monad-gods. If one reads the Old Testament, one will very quickly find that the term "God" is plural in Hebrew (Elohim) more than 85% of the time it is employed. Yet, it is surrounded by singular pronouns and other singular grammatical forms. This opens the door wide open for a unity in a diversity within God: the Trinity. Yet, if one opens a Watchtower magazine (Jehovah Witness), or the

Koran, or literature form the oneness groups, you will discover that they never reemploy that type of grammatical structure (single nouns joined to plural pronouns in a sentence) in their publications. Yet, when they appeal to the Old Testament, they are confronted with a unity and diversity within the sentence structure of the Bible. Thus, if one were to write a book describing a God who is Triune, one would employ the types of grammatical structure found in the Bible, a structure absent in the works of the monad religions.

Further problems arise because a monad god would depend on men and angels to fulfill some inner lack: love and communion. This unitarian god would lack love, communication, and equality in his essential nature and being. Without the attributes of love and fellowship, he could not even be a personal being. If this solitary god needed to create angels, jinn, or men (to give and receive love) that would imply that he depends on his creation. A dependent god is not God at all. Love, fellowship, equality, and personhood are essential to God's being. Only the biblical God has these attributes as essential to His being. God is God, and He does not depend on His creation for anything. Without people and cherubim, God would still love and have fellowship, and not lack anything. Francis Schaeffer rightly summed up the solution that the Trinity provides:

> The Nicene Creed—three persons, one God.
> ... Whether you realize it or not, that catapulted the Nicene Creed right into our century and its discussion: three Persons in existence, loving each other, and in communication with each other, before all else was. If this was not so, we would have had a God

who needed the universe as much as the universe needed God. But God did not need to create; God does not need the universe as the universe needs Him. Why? God is a full and true Trinity. The Persons of the Trinity communicated with each other before the creation of the world. This is not only an answer to the acute philosophic need of unity in diversity, but of personal unity and diversity. The unity and diversity cannot exist before God or behind God, because whatever is farthest back is God. ... The unity and diversity are in God Himself—three persons, yet one God. ... [T]his is not the best answer; it is the only answer. Nobody else, no philosophy, has ever given an answer for unity and diversity. ... Every philosophy has this problem, and no philosophy has an answer. Christianity does have an answer in the Trinity. The only answer to what exists is that He, the starting-place, is there.[13]

Allah, the one and only Allah, the eternal, absolute: he begetteth not, nor is He begotten (Sura 112).

No one has seen God at any time. The only begotten Son, who is in the bosom of the Father, He has declared Him (John 1:18).

But when the fullness of the time had come, God sent forth His Son, born of a woman, born under the law, to redeem those who were under the law, that we might receive

> the adoption as sons. And because you are sons, God has sent forth the Spirit of His Son into your hearts, crying out, "Abba, Father!" (Galatians 4:4-6).

Islam is a strict unitarian religion, whereby the supreme doctrine is the absolute and indivisible unity of Allah: *Al-Wahed*, the One (Sura 13:16, 74:11). Islam forbids the affirmation of God as Father. Allah is rigid, inflexible, unknowable, and capricious. One cannot have a personal relationship with Allah. Christ came to reveal the Father so that all His children can know God the Father through the Son by the Holy Spirit.

Halsey recognizes that the Triune God is "the key to genuine epistemology."[14] Non-Christian thought cannot supply the necessary preconditions for the rules of logic; thus, it is false. The contrary of the Trinity is impossible, and all non-Christian worldviews fall into absurdity because they cannot explain the universe and are self-contradictory. They lead to conclusions that contradict their own primary assumptions. Without the one God—the Father, the Son, and the Holy Spirit—nothing can make sense. The true and living God is the precondition for knowledge and the understanding all of human experiences, including the problem of the one and the many. One God in three persons is the inescapable truth.

> Go therefore and make disciples of all the nations, baptizing them in the name of the Father and of the Son and of the Holy Spirit (Matthew 28:19).

The former Agnostic, and Christian convert, Mortimer Adler said that "a God without mystery would be a projection of man, a man made god." C.S. Lewis said of God, the Trinity is a "thrilling mystery." Lewis further noted that space can move three ways:

- Left or right, backwards and forwards, or up and down. Every direction is either one of these or a compromise between them. They are called the three dimensions.
- A straight line: one dimension.
- A square: two dimensions.
- A cube: three dimensions.
- A world of one dimension would be a world of straight lines.
- In a two dimensional world, you still get straight lines but many make a figure.
- In a three dimensional world, you still get figures but many figures make one solid body.

Humans have souls that transcend this world but retain, and understand, the finite, three dimensional world. So, not only is the Trinity true; but God's word reveals God as the Father, Son, and Holy Spirit. In order to make sense out of anything in the world, we must have God as a precondition. In other words, as you advance to more real and more complicated levels, you do not leave behind the things you left or the simpler levels; you still have them, but combined in new ways, in ways you could not imagine, if you only knew the simpler levels. Human beings have souls that transcend this world, and yet retain and understand a three-dimensional world. Therefore, the diversity has unity; and the Trinity is true. God's word reveals God as Triune.

Why are there so many religions? Because, as Calvin

taught, man's heart is a *fabricum idolarum* (sorry, I love the way it sounds in Latin; it means an idol factory).

> The grace of the Lord Jesus Christ, and the love of God, and the communion of the Holy Spirit, be with you all. Amen (2 Corinthians 13:14).

Christianity: The Only Place Where Justice and Grace Meet

> Righteousness and justice are the foundation of His throne (Psalms 97:2).

> Now to him who works, the wages are not counted as grace but as debt. But to him who does not work but believes on Him who justifies the ungodly, his faith is accounted for righteousness (Romans 4:5-6).

I receive a traffic ticket for running a red light, and go to court. The judge asks, "What do you plead?" and I say, "Guilty, but I promise I will never break the traffic laws again. Judge, please forgive my ticket on account of my future obedience." The judge would say, "It is good that you will not break the law again. That is your obligation. But you still have to pay the fine for your past mistake of speeding." And all men are in a similar predicament before God: we are sinners in need of a pardon. The good news is that Jesus Christ, as judge, came down, took off His robe, and paid the fine for the sins of men.

All of the tens of thousands of religions, apart from one, believe that your future good works will help you get to heaven, nirvana, freedom from the karmic cycle or Paradise. Nonetheless, your good deeds can never erase your bad deeds. If you murder and rape five people, and later help feed three thousand people at a soup kitchen, you are still a murderer. If caught and tried, the good works will not rinse away your capital crimes. All men have sinned and they need an outside source to remove their sins. The unbeliever tries to deny this truth. The atonement expiates the sins of the Christian and rinses his transgressions from his spiritual record. Then, God graciously imputes Christ's righteousness to the believer's account. We enter heaven free from past sins and clothed in the righteousness of Christ through faith and by grace alone.

> To you first, God, having raised up His servant Jesus, sent Him to bless you, in turning away every one of you from your iniquities (Acts 3:26).

Justification: Pardon and Righteous Credit

> Mercy, it must be said that it is an attribute of God in the absolute sense of the word. God is rich in mercy, not because of or through any relation with us, but absolutely and in Himself.[15]

> Mercy triumphs over judgment (James 2:13).

Justification is by grace alone. It is a doctrinal term that is laid out in various books in the Bible. Justification, as a doctrine, is unique to Christianity. The doctrine of justification deems the believer as righteous, his sins are removed, and Christ's righteousness is accredited unto him by faith. No other religious schema has an agency by which to erase our report of errors and iniquity. Furthermore, they all fail to grant us a righteous record, so that we can enter a spotless heaven. Justification is a legal, forensic term that implies prior condemnation and results in complete acquittal and declaration of righteousness.

> Therefore, having been justified by faith, we have peace with God through our Lord Jesus Christ. ... For when we were still without strength, in due time Christ died for the ungodly. For scarcely for a righteous man will one die; yet, perhaps for a good man, someone would even dare to die. But God demonstrates His own love toward us, in that while we were still sinners, Christ died for us. Much more then, having now been justified by His blood, we shall be saved from wrath through Him (Romans 5:1-9).

The holy God of the universe demands a formal, unflawed righteousness, not because He is capriciously stern and demanding but because He is completely righteous. God is not whimsical; He is holy and perfect. One must be righteous to live with Him in heaven. Every man has broken God's holy law; the only solution for man's sin and depravity is a formal, legal justification through Christ.

> But to him who does not work, but believes on Him who justifies the ungodly, his faith is counted for righteousness (Romans 4:5).

Only Christianity can bestow justification. All the world's other religions are based upon the religionist's good deeds and personal merit. The problem is that heaven is perfect,

God is holy, and nothing unholy and unrighteous will enter God's heaven. Biblical justification is the only solution to man's sin and Adam's disobedience.

Imputation

> And he believed in the LORD; and He accounted it to him for righteousness (Genesis 15:6).

> But of Him you are in Christ Jesus, who became for us wisdom from God—and justification and sanctification and redemption (1 Corinthians 1:30).

The justified are given an alien righteousness, a righteousness that is not their own, but is imputed unto them by faith. Not having a righteousness of our own ensures that God gets all the glory. As Thomas Boston puts it, "We cry down the law, when it comes to our justification; but, we set it up, when it comes to our sanctification. The law drives us to the gospel that we are justified, and then sends us to the law again to show us our duty, now that we are justified."

> But You, O Lord, *are* a God full of compassion, and gracious, long-suffering and abundant in mercy and truth (Psalms 86:15).

- Justice is receiving what one deserves.

- Mercy is not receiving what one deserves.

- Grace is receiving what one does not deserve.

NOTES

1. Cornelius Van Til, *Defense of the Faith*, (P & R, Phillipsburg: PA, [1955], 1967), p. 12.
2. John Frame, *The Doctrine of the Knowledge of God*, (P & R, Phillipsburg: NJ, 1989), p. 175.
3. Van Til, *Survey of Christian Epistemology*, (P & R, Phillipsburg: NJ, 1969), p. 201
4. Greg Bahnsen, *Presuppositionalism*, (Covenant Media Foundation, Texarkana: Arkansas, January 1995), Penpoint Vol. VI:1.
5. Greg L. Bahnsen, *Always Ready*, (Covenant Media Foundation, Texarkana: Arkansas, 1996), p. 205.
6. Greg L. Bahnsen, *Van Til's Apologetic*, (P & R, Phillipsburg: NJ, 1998), p. 502.
7. Ronald H. Nash, *The Word of God and the Mind of Man*, (P & R, Phillipsburg: NJ, 1982), p. 59.
8. Edgar, p. 131.
9. Van Til, *Survey*, pp. 222-223.
10. John Owen *The Glory of Christ*, (Banner of Truth, Carlisle: PA, [1684], 2000), p. 66.
11. Robert Letham, *The Holy Trinity*, (P & R, Phillipsburg: NJ, 2004), p. 381.
12. Jonathan Edwards, S. Hyun Lee, Editor, *The Works of Jonathan Edwards Vol. 21*, (Yale Press, New Haven: CT), p. 114.
13. Francis Schaeffer, *Trilogy: He is There and He Is Not Silent*, (Crossway, Westchester: IL, 1990), pp. 288-289.
14. Jim S. Halsey, *For Such a Time as This* (P & R, Phillipsburg: NJ, 1976), p. 40.
15. Herman Hoeksema, *Reformed Dogmatics*, (Reformed Free Publications, Grand Rapids: MI, 1966), p. 115.

CHAPTER TWO
Islam: The Religion Of Allah

The word "Islam" is defined as submission, submission to Allah. Islam was birthed through the personality and the sword of Muhammad, who lived in Arabia from 570 to 633 A.D. Muhammad proclaimed that the angel Gabriel appeared to him in a cave near Mecca in 610 A.D. This alleged revelation from Allah through Gabriel to Muhammad is maintained to be the words of Allah. These words were recorded on bones, leafs, paper, skins, and other material and organized into the 114 Suras (chapters) of the Koran. A larger amount of additional material was recorded in the Hadith (accounts of the life and sayings of Muhammad).

Islam posits the notion that Allah can lie. That he is not bound to truth telling. Denying a universal while using particulars is more than difficult; and, the denial of a moral law prohibiting lying is self-defeating:

- q = The prohibition of lying is universal, nonmaterial, and necessary for communication.
- To deny q, it requires one to affirm q in that denial; the denial is self-defeating, and thus false.
- p = The Triune God: alone supplies the universal, nonmaterial, and necessary foundation for the perpetual prohibition of lying (Allah is not bound to a truth-telling moral nature).
- q therefore p. Yahweh's existence is mandatory.

If the Muslim denies this, another man only has to claim that he said the opposite. Thus, one could press every thesis as the antithesis.
Or, he could assert unremittingly that the Muslim is in fact a Mormon against the Muslim's heated protestations.

Islam offers a view of morality. There is a distinction between morality and moral law. Everyone and every religion has some type of morality, but moral law can only come from and be accounted for by one with exhaustive power, authority, and knowledge. These necessary attributes all autonomous humans and all human generated religion are deficient. Moral law is required for communication, yet religious anti-theism cannot supply the mandatory pre-necessities for it. This clearly undermines the notion of moral law in those systems, such as in Islam.

Moral law is required for communication because the Lord

God mandates that one should not lie. If this is not so, I could misstate what you state and assert that you said the opposite and antithesis of what you in fact did assert.

Muslims Stuck in a Vicious Circular Argument

A *pettio principii* is the logical fallacy of arguing in a circle: the conclusion of your argument also rests in your premise. The claim ends at the place it began. Christian theism avoids this fallacy inasmuch as it rests on transcendental necessities of God. But most Muslims argue that Allah is true because the Koran says so, and the Koran is true because Allah says so. They also try to prove the Koran by positing Muhammad and proving Muhammad by positing the Koran. That is a circular argument and circular arguments are invalid. Islam fails to deliver the transcendental necessities to avoid an invalid epistemic foundation.

Biblical Inerrancy

> And so we have the prophetic word confirmed, which you do well to heed as a light that shines in a dark place, until the day dawns and the morning star rises in your hearts; knowing this first, that no prophecy of Scripture is of any private interpretation, for prophecy never came by the will of man, but holy men of God spoke *as they were moved* by the Holy Spirit. And so we have the prophetic word confirmed, which you do well to heed as a light that shines in a dark place, until the day dawns, and the morning

star rises in your hearts; knowing this first, that no prophecy of Scripture is of any private interpretation, for prophecy never came by the will of man, but holy men of God spoke, as they were moved by the Holy Spirit (2 Peter 1:19-21).

The sufficiency...of the extant biblical manuscripts is not divorced from...the original manuscripts (Greg Bahnsen).

The Christian has an infallible word in the Bible and it reveals a saving Redeemer. Many Muslims attack the Bible, despite the fact that the Koran affirms the Old Testament and the New Testament. The Koran is alleged to be a collection of revelations from Allah. Muslims propagate that the Koran was perfect in heaven. However, the Hadith (authoritative inspired commentary and information regarding Muhammad) asserts that the Koran had many divergent and conflicting readings. The manner in which the Koran evolved into a standardized manuscript was not by divine intervention, but by the choice of men. Uthman proposed the Hafsah Manuscript should be the standard text of the Koran. He had it dispensed throughout the Middle East and had the variant copies destroyed. So, unlike the Bible, there is not a reasonable system to find the original text.

The Koran Cites the Bible as God's Word

The inability to think critically and logically or to draw a distinction becomes a casualty of our time. We will never come to the truth on serious matters of faith and belief, if we do not know how to think our way through those beliefs.₁

The Koran testifies in numerous places that the previous revelation (the Old Testament and Gospels) is the word of God; but, nowhere does the Bible testify of the truth and inerrancy of the Koran (obviously because it came first). The Koran affirms the Bible in the following verses:

> Suras: 66:6, 12; 48:29; 34:31; 35:31; 19:12; 12:111; 10:37; 9:111; 7:156-157; 6:154-157; 5:49, 113-114; 3:3, 48-53; 2:91.

The above mentioned verses formally end the debate between the authenticity of the Bible in contrast to the Koran. The Koran avouches the biblical text and the Bible disaffirms Islamic teaching. This is devastating to the particular notions of Islamic thought and doctrine. Based on its own book, Islamic theology cannot be true for it contradicts the book it cites as the word of God.

The Old Testament Copies Are the Word of God

(Much of the material, in this section on inerrancy, is gleaned from Dr. Greg Bahnsen's work that he contributed in the book *Inerrancy*, Norman Geisler, Editor. The valid expansion and implications of his labor I posit are to be credited to his work, and not my own. And any miscomputations and imprecisions that are contained below are mine and should not be attributed to Bahnsen.)

The Bible reveals that copies of the Book of Proverbs were kept pure and are the word of God since King Solomon was given a copy (Proverbs 25:1). Ezra apprises us that they had the Law of Moses hundreds of years after the original was first written by Moses (Kings 2:3). The proclamation that the word of God in the Torah was in their hand contained the present tense words: "are/is" (Nehemiah 8:8). The prophets Nehemiah and Ezra possessed copies that Scripture reckons as the word of God.

Jesus preached from copies of the Old Testament and He never doubted their genuineness and unimpeachable reliability (Matthew 12:3-5, 21:16). Likewise, Peter, Paul, and the other Apostles knew that the Tenach (Old Testament) is the word of God. Thus, in the first century, the Old Testament was the pure word of God. God's providential preservation of the copies insured that they were identical to the originals.

The New Testament Copies Present the Autographa

> The New Testament is the most widely attested ancient text that humanity possesses.[2]

There resides such a voluminous amount of copies of the New Testament ancient texts that we know what was written in the autographa. Josh McDowell expounds and proves this in his two volumes of *Evidence Demands a Verdict I and II*. But the critics assert that some manuscripts have inaccuracies and mistakes. Nevertheless the errors in thousands of copies are easy to find. Scholars have pointed out that scribal mistakes in the copies would be similar to writing out a sentence 4000 times and having errors scattered throughout that work. By comparing all the sentences, it is easy to find the correct and perfect reading. My clear dependence on Bahnsen's relevant thought is revealed with the following illustration:

G-O-D C-E-R-T-A-I-N-L-Y E-X-I-S-T-S T-H-E C-O-N-T-R-A-R-Y I-S I-M-P-O-S-S-I-B-L-E

If this sentence were written three or four thousand times, some errors would be dispersed in the sentences. The inaccuracies in them would be easy to discover through contrasting, comparing, and scrutinizing the sentences, as you overlap all of them. One could assemble a perfect sentence from the collection of the material.

Further expansion of Bahnsen's thought reveals that if one exchanges a "G" with a "D" in 15 of the sentences, the remaining 3985 establishes the correct letter. Then, exchange an "E" with one "I" in 125 copies; and through comparisons with the remaining 3875, we could discover the mistake. And one could do this with every sentence by matching, paralleling, contrasting, overlying, and scrutinizing every one of them. Consequently, the New Testament has copious numbers of copies. So, one can easily place them together, and overlap the manuscripts to find the autographa, the original manuscript.

Jesus announced: "These things I have spoken to you while being present with you. But the Helper, the Holy Spirit, whom the Father will send in My name, He will teach you all things and bring to your remembrance all things that I said to you" (John 14:25-26). This verse supplies the foundation for one to know that inerrancy was not restricted to the original manuscripts. We presuppose that God is sovereign and that His Holy Spirit inspired and secured the revelation of God. The contrary is not possible.

> Over and over again, we are confronted with the obvious fact that biblical writers made use of existing copies, with the significant assumption that their authority was tied to the original text of which the copies are a reliable reflection (Greg Bahnsen).
>
> All Scripture is given by inspiration of God, and is profitable for doctrine, for reproof, for correction, for instruction in righteousness (2 Timothy 3:16).

God has spoken and His true revelation is in the Bible alone. No other book can furnish the rational pre-necessities to examine any document. In order to probe, examine, question, and to ponder the authenticity of any alleged holy book, one is required to utilize the laws of logic and unmovable moral law. Only the Bible has the conceptual scheme and *a priori* rational web to account for these essential laws.

> The authority and usefulness of extant copies and translations of the Scriptures is apparent throughout the Bible: They reproduce the original, autographical text (Bahnsen).
>
> The Bible itself indicates that the copies...function authoritatively—and can be esteemed as God's own word to man. Remember that the autographical text (the words, the truth) is not the same as the autographical codex (the physical document). The codex contains the text in its ink and paper. Loss of the original codex does not

mean the loss of the text (Bahnsen).

The main presuppositions for biblical textual purity are:

- God has providential control over His revelation.
- God's word supplies the necessary preconditions for logic and fixed ethics that are required to test any text.

The New Testament names streets, sites, fields, courts, pools, places (that is, the pool of Siloam, the Field of Blood, Solomon's Porch, etc.) and towns, which were destroyed in 70 A.D. by the Romans, when they conquered and crushed Judea and its holy site, the Temple. The gospel writers speak of these locations as still standing, and describe details that only an eyewitness would know. This is very strong evidence that the New Testament books predate 70 A.D., when the Temple and countless sites were destroyed. It takes more than great faith to believe that most of the New Testament books were written many years after the events it records (90 A.D. and after). It takes strong-willed blind faith fueled by faulty presuppositions to believe such unsubstantiated claims.

The inspired writers of Scripture proclaim the authenticity of copies of the originals. King Josiah found a copy of the Torah and God declared that it was the pure word of God (2 Kings 22). "The book by the hand of Moses" was discovered and all the Old Testaments texts were true and pure. Bahnsen pressed Van Til's view, "If we presuppose a sovereign God, observes Van Til, we need no longer worry whether or not the transmission of Scripture is not altogether accurate."

The Trinity or Allah: A Real Conversation

Muslim: You believe in three Gods.

Mike: No. We believe in the Trinity. Can you define the Trinity?

Muslim: It is three Gods that are one God. It doesn't make sense.

Mike: No. That is not the proper definition of the God of the Bible. He is three persons in one God. He is not three gods in one God or three persons in one person. The Trinity is the doctrine that declares three persons in one God. This does not break the logical Law of Non-contradiction.

Muslim: Tell me what is one plus one plus one?

Mike: Well, the better question that I have for you: What is one times one times one?

Muslim: One.

Mike: Exactly. Not only is the Trinity logical, it is impossible for God not to be the Father, the Son, and the Holy Spirit, one God. Let me ask you a question: if God is just a monad, a single person God, where did love come from? Who did Allah love before he created the angels or men? Love needs an object. Allah and all monad deities cannot have love as a basic part of their nature. Only the Triune God of Scripture is true and living.

Muslim: Well, I can't answer your question right now.

Mike: Let me ask you another question, where did the notion of equality come from? We believe all men are created equal. We know there are perfectly equal triangles and perfectly equal lines in geometric theory. Moreover, we never see in our physical universe two lines or two triangles that are perfectly equal. Where did the notion of equality come from if we cannot see it in our material world? Within the tri-unity of God: The Father, the Son, and the Holy Spirit were and are coequal. That is the unchanging basis that man has for equality among humankind. Humanity is created in the image and likeness of the Triune God; thus, we have an objective standard for equality. With Allah, can you justify unchanging equality?

Muslim: I have never thought of that.

Mike: One last thing, all men have sinned. You and I have broken God's law. God is perfect, and heaven is perfect. How can a sinner get into a perfect Paradise? Only Jesus Christ has the solution in His atoning work on the cross. He died to rinse away the sins of His people, and true Christians have justification before heaven's court. That means my sins are taken away and Christ's perfect law keeping righteousness is imputed to me; it is credited to my spiritual account. If you died tonight would you go to heaven?

This man later converted to Christ.

Witnessing to Muslims

The main thrust of witnessing to a Muslim is for one to demonstrate that all men, including the Muslim, are under God's judgment from breaking the moral law. All are sinners and all need a Savior.

According to the standards of men, many Muslims are good and decent people. They love their families and try to improve society through hard work. Muslim terrorists are pure evil and most Muslims are not terrorists (yet, almost all terrorists are Muslims). The interesting aspect of this phenomenon is that the terrorists are trying to follow true Islam and its founder, Muhammad. The modern day Muslim terrorist aims to be faithful to Muhammad's life and instruction. Thus, Muhammad ordered the killing of many people and the Muslim terrorist engages in similar activity.

The Islamic moral code is an ethical system that sanctions death for verbal crimes and the repression of women. It is worth noting that if Allah is a lone monad deity, love could not be part of his eternal nature. Moreover, love is the heart and motivation of true morality. The Islamic god cannot account for love since it is not an eternal attribute of his nature. The biblical God is love. He has loved, through all eternity, as the Father loved the Son and the Holy Spirit. Love flows to man from God's nature because love is an eternal attribute of the true God. Islam recoils at the thought of God as Father, who offers free grace and eternal love to sinners. Much of ancient and modern Muslims profess that Allah is a god, who has commanded his followers to pursue jihad against Jews, Christians, and all other "infidels" (see Sura 2:193; 8:12, 17, 41, 60; 9:5, 14, 29, 123; and Hadith 1:25; 4:196, etc.). Remember that it was Muhammad himself, who led or ordered twenty-seven warring attacks against the "infidels." He, as their supreme lawgiver, gave the order to decapitate 900 Jewish men for opposing him and not receiving him as a prophet.

Millions of Muslims avouch and support jihad. Jihad against Israel, America, and all non-Muslims is an important element in the worldview of large populations of Muslim people. The Koran commands: "Slay the idolaters, wherever you find them...ambush them" (Sura 9). The Arabic dictionary defines jihad: "To fight and kill in the path of Allah, the enemies of Allah, for the cause of Allah. It can also be used to mean to strive in the path of Allah."

Muslim Duty

Muhammad launched and advanced Islam with the sword. Muhammad himself led numerous invasions on neighboring villages during his lifetime, while his followers engaged in fifty more. Many times the conquered people were given the choice of conversion to Islam or death. Christians, pagans, and Jews were killed by the armies of Muhammad in seventh century Islam. Islam's inception is associated with war. At Islam's birth, there were eighty-three military campaigns involving Muslims.

Muhammad spearheaded or ordered almost eighty attacks. Jesus Christ and all His apostles ordered zero military attacks. Islam is a warring religion, and has been so in every century it has existed. Even George Washington had to deal with Islam's warring and plundering. Muslims were kidnapping Americans and receiving large ransoms for the captured. President Washington wrote a letter in 1786 to Marquis de Lafayette, complaining of Muslim terrorism, and wished that America "had a navy able to reform those enemies of mankind, or crush them into nonexistence."

Muhammad engaged in many dozens of armed battles. The Apostle Paul commanded zero military campaigns. Muhammad organized over five dozen raids. Peter, Paul, John, James, Mark, and all the Christians for the first three hundred years of Christianity, directed zero military wars. Muhammad stirred up hatred and conducted numerous conquests in the name of Allah.

Muslim Nonstop Warfare

> Would you rather have an Allah, who demands that you kill me so you can go to heaven, or a Jesus, who says to love Him and others because you are going to heaven? (Rick Mathes).

The conquest of Constantinople, in 1453, saw Christians massacred and cut down like grass by Muslim invaders.

Christian diplomats, citizens, ministers, women, and children were butchered. Bodies were stacked up as high as the wall around the city. The churches were converted to Mosques, as several thousand of massacred heads bobbed in the bay. The Muslims were motivated by jihad and dreams of a world-wide Islamic conquest.

> Hear, O Muslims, the meaning of life. The peak of the matter is Islam itself. The pillar is *Rakatin* prayer. And the topmost part is jihad - holy war (Muhammad in the Hadith).

Christianity the Source of Human Rights: Islam a Source of Abuse

> They have lived long and prospered. But now, we shall invade their land and curtail their borders (Koran, Sura 21:41-46).

> Muhammad asked, "Isn't the witness of a woman equal to half of that of a man?" The women replied, "Yes." He said, "This is because of the deficiency of the woman's mind" (Haddith, Volume 3:826).

Early Christianity grew and spread by the spoken word, peace, love, and sacrifice; it overtook the whole Roman Empire by persuasion and works of compassion. Islamic morality is the antithesis of Christian morality. Islam spread by ambush, atrocities, and forced conversions. Last century, this warring religion murdered a million and a half Armenian Christians in Turkey. It is against the law to publicly preach a non-Islamic religion in every Muslim nation. The death penalty is imposed on all those who are found guilty of this "offense."

Islam lacked a common usage word for "heresy until the nineteenth century."3 Lewis adds that the "main difference between the Sunnis and the Shi`a, whose theological differences are minimal, often diverge considerably on point of law."4 Thus, they kill each other and have for over ten centuries over religious disputes. All violent religionists should affirm and embrace the Christian worldview of love, lawfulness, and peace.

> Allah's messenger has commanded: fight against the unbelievers and kill them. Pursue them until even a stone would say; come here Muslim, there is an infidel hiding. Kill him. Kill him quickly (Koran, Sura 16:13).

The former section is just a brief recounting of Islam's history. It is stunning and a little scary. However those are just evidential and historical arguments. The main problem for Islam is it has a fallacious epistemology (the basis for all knowledge). That is, my dominant argument can function to undermine Islam's relation to its false and irrational epistemology. The Muslim cannot account for logic, love, absolute morals, and knowledge.

Islam Nullifies Itself

> The true God is one in nature but has many attributes and exists in three persons (the Father, the Word, and the Holy Spirit); whereas the god of Islam is one only, the many different names or attributes that are assigned to him are merely nominal, that is, they are descriptions of

his will, and not at all characteristics that are essential to his ontology or being. Allah "is utterly incomparable."[5]

The god proposed by Islam is a self-nullifying concept. According to Islam, Allah is above and beyond all distinction. He is absolutely and completely one in every aspect of his being. There is nothing that can compare to Allah or is analogous to him. Consequently, he cannot be a person or a known entity. For, if he has personality or is a person, then he shares something in common with men. If you say that he is a nonpersonal entity or a thing, then he has many items in common with things. In short, Allah is not a person or a thing, as taught in Islam. Allah is ascribed as wholly and completely incomparable, transcending and beyond all things, as there is nothing that is analogous about him. Correspondently, he then cannot be anything, and he is nothing. Something which cannot be a thing is nothing, and cannot exist by definition.

Muslim dogma adds to its anti-theistic problems in asserting that the Koran is the revelation of an eternal book located in Paradise. If Allah is the only eternal being, and nothing exists that is analogous to him, nothing can share anything in common with him in his being and attributes; hence, an eternal book in Paradise cannot exist. Thus the Koran is not a revelation from a god, it fails to be what it reveals it is. It is a self-refuting and fallacious book. It drills a hole in its own boat of reason.

How to Witness to Muslims: Simple but Powerful

> Jesus said to him, "I am the way, the truth, and the life. No one comes to the Father ex-

cept through Me" (John 14:6).

The first truth that must be presented to a Muslim (or a person of any religion) is the law of God. Before one proclaims grace one must inform the nonbeliever of his sin problem. Jesus commanded: "Therefore you shall be perfect, just as your Father in heaven is perfect" (Matthew 5:48). Perfection is required to be accepted by God and to make it into heaven. The unbeliever must know that this is the standard and not human goodness. He must be told of his sin and that he, as have all humans, has transgressed God's law and broken the Lord's commandments. This provokes a desire for the grace and love the Savior alone provides.

Muslims contend that Allah is merciful, but he gives mercy without justice. Since Allah offers forgiveness, but disregards justice, he is not just. The true God is both merciful and just. He demands justice based on His righteousness, but He offers a saving Savior in Christ, who supplies forgiveness based on His death on the cross. Both justice and grace are provided in the atonement of Jesus.

Jesus: The Truth

> Prediction is hard, especially when it's about the future (Yogi Berra).

Jesus is the Truth. The Koran instructs "Seek knowledge, in China, if necessary" (Sura 39:12). One should go where the evidence leads. There were 333 Prophecies about the coming Messiah written in the Old Testament before the birth of Christ. All these came true in the birth, life, death, and resurrection of Jesus of Nazareth. No other religious leader or prophet ever had massive predictive material written about their life before their birth. Jesus had countless fulfilled predictions about His life to attest to His claims as the Son of God. His virgin birth was predicted several hundred years before He was born. Islam attempts to twist three or four Scriptures in an attempt to verify Muhammad's claims. The Mormons attempt to misinterpret five or six Scriptures for the same reason in regard to Joseph Smith. Jesus did not have five or six; He had hundreds of clear and unambiguous prophecies that predicted events in His life before they occurred, even hundreds of years before His birth. Jesus also predicted numerous prophecies for the first century (Matt. 24, Revelation, etc.). They all came true.

If a claimant comes and announces that He's a god or the way to God, he should provide some evidence. Jesus Christ came and provided *a posteriori* proof by fulfilling numerous predictions. Powerful evidence would be for a man to claim that he is from God, and before he arrived, there were preexisting documents written before he was born, which contained hundreds of details that were forecast about his future life. Later, these specific facts were fulfilled in his life. That is powerful *a posteriori* and mathematical evidence. Christ fulfilled numerous prognostications and they were not vague and general. If that was so easy to produce, why hasn't anyone else started a religion, which provided hundreds of fulfilled predictions to demonstrate divine prescience? The reason is obvious; no one has the ability but the Triune God.

The prophet Micah foretold that the Messiah would be born in Bethlehem; Isaiah portended the type of birth that He was to have (Isaiah 7:14); Psalms 22 predicted His death on the cross, as did Isaiah 53. The prophet Daniel, in chapter nine, predicted the day that Christ arrived in Jerusalem. Isaiah in the ninth chapter prerecorded Christ's Godhood. Many more events, people, places, and times were prearranged by Yahweh and made known to men and documented before the events occurred.

Christ's coming: the place, date, type of events were predicted on copies of the Old Testament dated centuries before Christ arrived with extra-biblical sources verifying much of the details of His life and death. Noteworthy is the fact that Jesus could not self-fulfill most of these prophecies unless He was the sovereign God.

> The Father loves the Son, and has given all things into His hand. He who believes in the Son has everlasting life; and he who does not believe the Son shall not see life, but the wrath of God abides on him (John 3:35-36).

Only Christ has Risen

Frank Morrison, a lawyer, disdained Christianity so much that he set out to write a book disproving the resurrection of Christ. After months of research, digging, studying, reading, examining the evidence, he fell on his knees and trusted Jesus Christ as Lord. For the evidence, contrary to his stated goals, was overwhelming. He discovered that the proof for Christ was unassailable. He did write a book, titled *Who Moved the Stone?* and subtitled, *The Book that Refused to be Written*. Harvard law professor, Simon Greenleaf, wrote the text book on legal evidence, which was used for over a hundred years in American law schools. His tome taught the proper manner in which one ought to measure and discern evidence in court. Greenleaf was a skeptic and unremittingly blasted Christianity in his law classroom. One day, a student challenged him to investigate the evidence for the resurrection of Jesus. He searched the evidence, examined it, investigated it, and became a Christian. The evidence for the Messiah was overwhelming to the expert on evidence. All the founders of the multitudes of religions, once deceased, remain deceased, including Muhammad. Unlike any other, Jesus Christ rose from the grave.

Islam's main motif for denying the doctrine of the resurrection of Christ is to claim that Jesus never died. Since he did not die, He never rose from the grave. That notion goes against all the eyewitness testimony and it is a very weak volley. Even Christ's contemporary enemies did not dispute His death.

Crucifixion and a Resurrection

A woman wrote to a radio minister and said, "Our teacher said that on Good Friday, Jesus just swooned on the cross and that His Disciples nursed Him back to health. What do you think?" The minister replied, "Dear sister, beat your teacher with a leather whip for 39 heavy strokes. Nail him to a cross. Hang him in the sun for six hours. Run a spear through his heart. Embalm him. Put him in an airless tomb for three days, and then see what happens." Jesus was crucified and now He is alive. The tombs of all the others are full of dead man's bones.

God will not unjustly wave off your sins. It would be immoral if a civil judge just waves people's crimes away and decrees that a dozen murderers and rapists are forgiven because he wants to set them free. We would say that the judge is not good, and that he is unconscionable. Muslims claim Allah can arbitrarily forgive their sins without justice being carried out. This is outrageous and false. The true and living God is just and righteous. Only through Christ's death on the cross can mercy as well as justice be satisfied. An eternal Messiah paying the price for our sins against an eternal God is the only solution for sin and depravity.

> A six-pointed star, a crescent moon, a lotus—symbol or other religious symbols suggest beauty and light. The symbol of Christianity is an instrument of death. It suggests hope.6

> Few have lived to equal John the Baptist. His blows fell with a thud and a sharp edge that shook the oaks of Bashan. ... The modern counterpart is seen as an improvement on the rough and heavy one that John used. It is lighter and more highly polished...and much easier to swing...but what sort of trees can it fell? When John wielded his axe...he made chips fly. That rough-looking man...who ate no dainties...produced trembling in the hearts of the people and a confessing of their sins. This is the need of the times: men of God, skilled in the use of the ax of the Word (Franklin Ferguson).

The Muslim must first understand the judgment that awaits him without the Savior Jesus. Paul understood this: "Knowing, therefore, the terror of the Lord, we persuade men" (2 Corinthians 5:11). Christians are called to raise the law above the heads of non-Christians in order to create desperation and the knowledge that they must have grace through the gospel. The Psalmist announced: "The law of the LORD is perfect, converting the soul" (Psalms 19:7). The Apostle Paul reminded us that "by the law is the knowledge of sin" (Romans 3:20). After the terror of the law is made known to the non-Christian, the believer is then to offer the comfort of the gospel: "For I am not ashamed of the gospel of Christ, for it is the power of God unto salvation to everyone who believes" (Romans 1:16). And the gospel is: "Moreover, brethren, I declare to you the gospel...by which also you are saved...that Christ died for our sins according to the Scriptures, and that He was buried, and that He rose again the third day" (1 Corinthians 15:1-4). Thereupon share with the Muslim the bad news and then offer him the good news.

Below is a typical conversation when a Christian witnesses to a Muslim:

> Mike: Hey, how's it going? Can I talk to you about God?
>
> Manny: Fine and sure.
>
> Mike: Do you believe in God?
>
> Manny: Well, I'm a Muslim.
>
> Mike: That's an interesting religion. I'm a Christian and as a Christian, I know I have sinned and transgressed God's commandments and messed up. Do you ever sin?
>
> Manny: Of course, every day. Everyone does.

Mike: How do you find forgiveness?

Manny: Allah forgives me.

Mike: How, and on what basis, does he forgive you?

Manny: His mercy.

Mike: If it's mercy without justice, then that's not an answer. For you and I have lied. We have cheated, lusted, and we have committed all kinds of crimes against a holy God. And you and I will go to hell for ever, if we do not have our sins removed through an atonement. The Bible says that there is no remission of sins without the shedding of blood. You and I have not always respected our elders, those in authority; you and I have been untruthful and have fallen into lust at times. So, we are doomed without atonement. Only Jesus Christ died on the cross for our sins. You need to turn from your ways and trust in Christ and have your sins removed.

Manny: I'm a good person. I do my best.

Mike: Well, according to God's law, I'm not a good person and I have never met one. And you have admitted that you have sinned. Have you ever stolen anything? Have you ever taken extra napkins or catsup form a fast-food restaurant? Have you ever lusted?

Manny: Of course, everyone has.

Mike: Then you are a lying, lusting thief, who desperately needs a Savior. Jesus is the only one who died on the cross for our sins. Repent and come to Christ today or go to an endless punishment.

Manny: I'll have to think about it. Here's my e-mail address. Let me know about going to church with you sometime this month.

Our Witness for Christ

When witnessing to a Muslim, the Christian is to be faithful to Scripture. This demands that one set the law of God on the sinner, before the offer of the grace of God through the gospel. Reisinger amplifies this use of God's law:

> The biblical answer is that God requires personal, perfect, perpetual obedience to His revealed will...that...is summarized in the Ten Commandments. ... The Commandments demand both external and internal obedience.[7]

The veracity of man's rebellion against God's holy law is to be brought before the eyes of the unbeliever to both convince and convict him of his sins. Using clear, specific, and particular commandments, in asserting the sinner's pollution before a holy God, is the first stage of faithful witnessing. This is the instrument one should use to humble him, and provoke a sense of misery and wretchedness that will drive him to Jesus for cleansing, forgiveness, and redemption.

Faithful witnessing to the Muslim consists of the believer heralding the judgment of the law on the lost, and then offering the grace of the gospel to those without Christ. Christians are not to preach a controllable god, a god who is only there to meet the unbeliever's needs. Such a god becomes a divine vending machine who must dispense stuff at our call. Much of the Christian world seems to be embarrassed by the true God, and they try to change Him into a more user-friendly deity. An almighty sovereign God, full of awe and righteousness, is not what the world wants. But He is the God all people need. The Bible reveals that "the fear of the Lord is the beginning of wisdom" (Proverbs 9:10). Christians should press God's law on the Muslim with compassion and patience. We are not to dazzle them with rhetoric or blast them with an uncaring scolding. One must warn them. We should sincerely care for the state of their souls through the graceful preaching of the law and the gospel.

The foremost reason one should esteem Christianity over Islam is that the Bible predates the Koran by many hundreds of years and there is not one passage in the Koran that claims the Bible is unreliable, changed or corrupted. There are numerous verses in the Koran that reckon the Bible as true and that it is the word of God. Islam's holy book esteems the Bible as God's word and the Bible was written before the Koran. The two books disagree on God's nature and the path of salvation. Clearly one should take the Bible over the Koran.

The Only Authentic Holy Book

1. The Bible ascribes a different nature for

God, and a completely dissimilar way and means to salvation than Islam.
2. The Koran affirms the Bible (Muhammad directed Christians to follow the Bible they had in the seventh century in Koran verses: 2:40-42, 89,126; 3:3,71, 93; 4:47; 5:47-51, 69-72; 6:91; 7:157; 29:45,46; 35:31).
3. The Bible is correct on the nature of God and salvation, not the Koran.

Precious Promises

> As His divine power has given to us all things that pertain to life and godliness, through the knowledge of Him who called us by glory and virtue, by which have been given to us exceedingly great and precious promises, that through these you may be partakers of the divine nature, having escaped the corruption that is in the world through lust (2 Peter 1:3-4).

Islam along with every false religion has one basic miscalculation in touching salvation: Its followers are trying to reach God, find God, and please God through their Good works, sacraments, rituals, and jumping through the right religious hoops.

Christianity is God reaching down to man. Christianity claims that Christians have not found God, but that God found them. God decreed the directive for the Son of God to descend from Heaven to live and then die on the cross to pardon the sins of His people. Man centered religion cringes at this thought. It insists that we try to be good enough. It tries to put its followers on religious treadmills. Laboring to do those proper religious works and to clean up one's soul is no real solution. Why would one want to accept Muhammad's word that the angel Gabriel spoke to him from Allah and reject Christianity? It does not make any sense to reject the foundation and source of logic that also supplies complete everlasting absolution and acceptance by God.

> There are some who trouble you, and want to pervert the gospel of Christ. But even if we, or an angel from heaven, preach any other gospel to you than what we have preached to you, let him be accursed. As we have said before, so now I say again, if anyone preaches any other gospel to you than what you have received, let him be accursed (Galatians 1:7-9).

Every false religion, pronounced by false prophets, lacks the capacity to clean up anyone's spiritual record of sin. Only Jesus can, that is why Jesus came to earth, to love and to die. Self-centered religion tries to conform and reform to earn salvation. Jesus Christ transforms through real forgiveness and the empowerment by the Holy Spirit. Therefore false deities cannot provide complete forgiveness and eternal hope. Morey sums up the problems of Islam: "What we have said is that while the Koran claims that Allah is God and Muslims think they are worshipping the one true God, in reality they are worshipping a false god preached by a false prophet according to a false book."

Question for Muslims

Considering that Islam claims that Muhammad is the last and greatest prophet, it is illogical that the Koran asserts the following concerning Jesus Christ in contrast to Muhammad:

- Jesus was born of a virgin (Sura 19:16-35): not Muhammad.
- Jesus is the Messiah (Sura 4:171): not Muhammad.
- Jesus is a Spirit from God (Sura 4:171): not Muhammad.
- Jesus is the Word of God (Sura 4:171): not Muhammad.
- Jesus was sinless (Sura 19:19): not Muhammad.
- Jesus gave life to the dead. (Sura 3:49 and 22:73): not Muhammad.
- Jesus is coming back again as a sign of the hour of judgment (Sura 43:61): not Muhammad.
- Jesus performed many miracles (Sura 3:49 and 100:110): not Muhammad (Sura 29:47-51).

There is something very special about Jesus Christ. No other prophet or false prophet has His divine nature and accomplished what He did and taught what He taught (John 1:1, 10:30, 5:18, 8:24, 8:58, 20:28; 1 Timothy 3:16; Col. 1:16-17, 2:9; Matt. 22:42-45; Mark 14:64). Buddha, Joseph Smith, Krishna, Sun Yung Moon, and Muhammad never did what Jesus Christ did. Jesus died for our sins and rose again on the third day. He performed many miracles. He claimed to be God and demonstrated His deity.

Growth through Love and Truth

Jesus promised that His Church would grow from a small mustard seed to a world wide movement and it has: from eleven followers to billions of Christians in every country in the world. The movement of Jesus, Christianity, grew large and fast by the power of love, truth, peace, and self-sacrifice. Islam grew by the sword. Muhammad and his followers killed many Jews, Christians, and Pagans as they plundered their towns. Islam advanced by the use of force: Christianity through love. Christians believe in a God of love; of the 99 names of Allah in the Koran, he is never called the God of love or Father. The name of the true and living God, which the Jews and the Christians worshipped in pre-Islamic Arabia, was Rahman in Arabic. Not Allah. Allah was the name of the moon god among the 360 deities in Mecca that the Pagans worshipped. The Meccan Pagans also practiced many of the rituals and ceremonies that Islam practices at the Kaaba. History proves that before Islam came into existence, the Sabeans worshipped the moon god, Allah, who married the sun god and had three daughters. In the 1950's the moon god temple was unearthed at Hazor. Two idols of this god were found, proving Allah was a pre-Islamic pagan deity.

Jesus is the Messiah: the Christ. We can examine a pre-Christian and pre-Islamic source (not the New Testament or the Koran) to find the definition of the Messiah: the Old Testament. It, including the Torah, proclaims that the Messiah would be God (Psalms 110; Isaiah 7:14, 9:6, 43;10-11; Genesis 1:26, 3:22; Zechariah 10:12,12:10; Dan. 7:13-14; etc.). Jesus is the Messiah (John 4), so Jesus of Nazareth is the Messiah and is God (also see Revelation 1:7-8; 22:7 and 13; Hebrews 1).

The Koran informs us that Muhammad had to repent of sins (Sura 40:55, 47:19, 48:1-2, 33:36-38). Jesus did not sin. Jesus was affirmed sinless by the combative religious leaders of His day; the Romans said he was sinless; the traitor Judas asserted that Jesus was sinless; and those who lived with Jesus for three years professed that He had never sinned. Adam, Moses, Abraham, David, and Jonah all sinned (Sura 2:36, 7:22-23, 26:82, 28:15-16, 37:142, 38:24-25). Only Jesus was and is sinless. He died on the cross for the atonement of believers; no other religion has provided an eternal atonement. Heaven is perfect and men are not; men must have their sins expiated. All mortals require an all powerful atonement to enter heaven. All men need their sins atoned for, only Christianity has an infinite atonement. Christ's sacrifice and resurrection justifies those who repent and trust Him. One can have legal, forensic righteousness to enter into the perfect purity of heaven, or reject Christ and attempt to live a religious life that cannot remove your past sins.

The Harshness of the Law Leads One to a Savior

> The Book of good deeds and bad deeds will be set before you; and you will set the sinful in great terror because of what is therein; they will say, "Woe to us! What a book is this! It leaves out nothing small or great, but takes account thereof" (Sura 18:49).

> Therefore, having been justified by faith, we have peace with God through our Lord Jesus Christ. ... For when we were still without strength, in due time Christ died for the un-

> godly. For scarcely for a righteous man will one die; yet, perhaps for a good man, someone would even dare to die. But God demonstrates His own love toward us, in that while we were still sinners, Christ died for us (Romans 5:1-8).

The doctrine of justification by grace is absent from Islam. Islam stresses that the balance of one's righteous deeds must outweigh their unrighteous deeds in order to "attain salvation" in Paradise. Those whose unrighteous works outweigh their righteous works are doomed to hell (Sura 23:102-3). In Christianity, justification is by grace alone. Justification is a forensic term laid out in various books in the Bible. Since Christianity alone supplies true forgiveness and justification, one only has to remind the person who follows another religion that they are a sinner before you extend the relief of the gospel. The zealous preacher, Robert M'Cheyne, offered this inspiring quote: "If the mercies and if the judgments do not convert you, God has no other arrows in His quiver." The terror and thunder of Sinai will invoke fear in the sinner. Then, if God changes the sinner's heart through the gospel, the convert will flee God's judgments and hurl himself upon Christ and His eternal mercy.

> I say to you that likewise, there will be more joy in heaven over one sinner who repents than over ninety-nine just persons who need no repentance (Luke 15:7).

When one shares the love of God without preaching God's exactness in law, it weakens the sinners' sense of sin. Then the lost sinner is not interested in the grand truth of the cross and justification. The law and the gospel, these are the means God uses to save lost sinners through His Spirit. Soteriological truth's summation is "to know nothing but Christ and Him crucified." God is the righteous King, whom all men have offended in every point of His holy law, and Christ the Savior died for our transgressions, of that very same law.

The Impossibility Of Islam: A Transcendental Critique

> I think it hard to see how Islam, or for that matter, any religion based on belief in a unitary god, can possibly account for human personality or explain the diversity in unity of the world.[8]

A unitarian god does not possess the eternal diversity in his nature to account for the diverse and necessary laws (the Law of Non-contradiction distinct from the Law of Identity, and the particulars in moral law) and the particulars in the cosmos (people and things). Islamic theology cannot account for nor explain the problem of unity in diversity (the one and many). Letham opines that Islam is a "militant and monolithic unifying principle, with no provision for diversity."[9] A uni-personal being lacks the capacity to account for eternal and temporal particulars.

> Allah is utterly incomparable.[10]

> He (Yahweh) is all-determining and irresistible power, but also a caring parent. He is not contingent (that is, dependent) on the world, but neither is he 'removed from the

> contingencies of the world,' for He is very much involved in the world he has made. He...abounds in love and responsiveness, generosity, and sensitivity. He is a person, not merely a metaphysical principle.[11]

Allah is not inalterably and ontologically just, merciful or moral, he only inscribes attributes to himself for communication purposes (Sura 6:12). Allah is not faithful, merciful, and loving because these attributes are not an aspect of his being; furthermore, Allah is not bound to goodness, righteousness, faithfulness, and love. He can decide to speak falsehoods and do evil. He has no true being or personality. One can know his decrees and his acts, but not his non-being, his non-person. Additionally one cannot provide that which one does not possess, ergo Allah is not a god of love, truth, and relationship.

Allah is alleged to be utterly transcendent (*tanzih*) and unknowable by humans. But if Allah is unknowable, how can the Koran reveal anything about him? Can one call Allah a him? An unknowable and unidentifiable strict unitarian god cannot be the indispensable foundation for the unity of experience and knowledge. Van Til warns that "the only alternative to thinking of God as the ultimate source of unity in human experience, as it is furnished by laws or universals, is to think that the unity rests in a void. Every object of knowledge must, therefore, be thought of as being surrounded by ultimate irrationality."[12] If one denies the Triune God, the world must be encircled by irrationality, but that is not possible. Islam's doctrine of god leaves room "neither for diversity, diversity in unity, nor a person grounding creation, for Allah is a solitary monad with unity only."[13] Islam clearly and completely denies the Trinity and so it falls into self-contradiction on its own ground. Even its fallacious assertions and false notions presuppose the truth of the Triune God.

- Islam fails to supply transcendental necessities.
- Without transcendental necessities Islam cannot account for knowledge.
- There must be knowledge.
- Islam is false.

Transcendental Analysis Defeats the Anti-theism of Islam

"Come now, and let us reason together," says the LORD (Isaiah 1:18).

Allah cannot supply the necessary presuppositions for knowledge. Allah cannot supply universals, thus he cannot make sense of the particulars in human experience. That is the reason Van Til promulgated that one must presuppose the Triune God, "not merely another fact of the universe."[14] This includes a singular god who lacks diversity.

The unadorned biblical argument is: Without Yahweh, one cannot account for anything, including the claims of various religionists. God, the Father, Son, and Holy Spirit, is the precondition for logic, morality, mathematics, and everything else in the cosmos. This is an undeniable and certain argument that is necessarily true. There is nothing that a disbeliever can avouch without ultimately relying on Christian Triune theism, since the immutable God alone provides the preconditions for the laws of logic. Thus, the Islamic anti-theist's argument will always presuppose the true God, the very one whom Islam rejects, because Islam cannot supply the preconditions for the unified diverse laws of logic, morality, and universals. The Triune God is the preexisting foundation for all debate. Deny the Trinity and one cannot debate anything, including religion.

No god, but The God

The allotheists must presuppose the biblical God as they argue against Him. "The existence of the God of Christian theism is presupposed by all rational thought and behavior."[15] Men are mortal and dependent. The true God is transcendent and necessary. "If God is the covenant head, then He is exalted above His people; He is transcendent."[16] One must have a fixed, timeless, and transcendent ground for knowledge. The human mind is too limited, temporal, and mutable to be the basis for knowledge. Anti-Triune theism and all thought presuppose Christian theism inasmuch as the Triune God alone provides the transcendental conditions necessary for rationality and knowledge. Christianity must be true; the contrary is impossible.

The biblical argument is compelling and certain. To attempt to argue against it would be like attempting to clear a velvet table covered with diamonds by adding more diamonds to the table. The new stones do not reduce the size or the weight of the collage of brilliance, they only add to it. Likewise, the arguments from anti-Triune theists only build more into the biblical argument because they have to utilize rational laws and ethics in their attempt to make their case. Since only the Trinity can confer the needed preconditions for distinct laws of logic, yet they are stuck using them, all their arguments presuppose Christianity and just add more weight and strength to it. Stern confessed that the attraction of transcendental arguments is that they "undercut the ground which the skeptical worries are built."17 Non-Trinitarian religions cannot intellectually dole out the foundation for the laws of logic that they are required to employ every time they assert anything about religion or human experience.

> The Law of Non-contradiction presupposes transcendental reasoning because there is no other way to justify the Law of Non-contradiction than transcendentally. The only way to argue for or against the Law of Non-contradiction is by relying on it. The Law of Non-contradiction is the precondition for our very ability to discuss its validity or invalidity. This is transcendental reasoning. As said, the Law of Non-contradiction presupposes the Christian God and worldview in particular. No other worldview can account for the transcendental necessity of logic, for no other worldview can account for universal, invariant, abstract entities, or why they apply to the realm of contingent changing experience. Only the infinite, eternal, unchangeable God, who made and governs everything in accordance with His rational character and plan, and who revealed Himself in the Scriptures of the Old and New Testaments, can provide the preconditions for the way all of us do and must approach the world (Anthony Rogers).

The truth of the biblical God's existence is not probable; it is certain. God's existence is the absolute precondition for all our questions and even all our doubts. We utilize logic in our questions as well as in our doubts, thereby affirming that God lives. Christianity is the only worldview that provides human reason a foundation for its proper function. Non-Christian systems of thought cannot furnish a foundation for the Law of Non-contradiction; thus, those systems of thought can only offer self-contradictory worldviews. Unless one believes in the Triune God, one cannot account for human experience. God is the precondition for all argument, proof, evidence, and reason. All human thought requires the employment and assumption of the universal and invariant laws of logic. Only the transcendent and unchanging God provides the necessary preconditions for the use of transcendent and unchanging laws of logic. To argue at all, one must presuppose that the God of Abraham, Isaac, and Jacob exists.

Knowledge is obtained by more than observation, experiments, and measurements. One has to apply the *a priori* rational tools to understand and interpret the data observed by sense perceptions. Some of these tools are the laws of logic. These laws are necessary and without them all other assumptions about anything become impossible. Deny the laws (plural): the Law of Identity and the Law of Non-contradiction (unity in diversity) and knowledge along with communication are not possible.

Anti-theism Rejects Truth

Nothing that is true that one can aver will contradict Christianity. The God of the Bible has all the answers, and without God no one would have a justified answer to any question. Jesus announced that He was "the truth." He is the truth, and the Holy Spirit is the Spirit of truth. To make any consistent and true statement, one must base it on the God of truth. Anything written or spoken that attempts to contradict and overturn the Lord's revelation is self-defeating and fallacious. We know that we are not just random accidents produced from a primordial and impersonal Big Bang. An explosion does not have order. The universe does have order, thus we are no accident. We call living things organisms. An organism presupposes organization and structure as well as a unity in diversity which Allah lacks. Without God in Trinity one could not account for the logic needed in creating a hypothesis. Islamic anti-theism and anti-theism in any form is self-contradicting and self-terminating.

Christian Theism is Inescapable

> As far as the east is from the west, so far has He removed our transgressions from us (Psalms 103:12).

Only Christianity can supply epistemic certainty and salvatory certainty. The truth of the Bible must be presupposed as fixed and certain. It is impossible for Christian theism to be false. It is more certain than the premise that all bachelors are unmarried. This is certain. Equally certain are the doctrines that Christ provides salvation freely and keeps those He saves. Through the cross, God removes the believer's sins as far as the east is from the west. If one lived in San Diego and wanted to travel as far west as possible, where would he go? When he started out west he could land in Hawaii, but the Philippines are still west of that, from the Philippines he could go west to China, and from there France, and then further west to New York and back to San Diego. How far west must he travel to reach the east? It is immeasurable and infinite. And so are his transgressions removed as he trusts in Christ. His transgressions are infinitely eliminated by the infinite atonement through the cross. That is good news that the Muslim faith and all other religions cannot deliver.

> Behold the Lamb of God who takes away the sin of the world (John 1:29).

All people require a spiritual cleansing. Only Jesus Christ and His death on the cross can wash away all their sins. Jesus died and rose again. No one else has done that for you. Van Til presses: "If God was to continue communication with His creature, it was either to be by condemnation or by atonement." God through His mercy provided a perfect and effectual atonement through the death of Jesus Christ on the cross. Believe on Him and you will be saved.

> But when the kindness and the love of God our Savior toward man appeared, not by works of righteousness, which we have done, but according to His mercy He saved us, through the washing of regeneration and renewing of the Holy Spirit, whom He poured out on us abundantly through Jesus Christ our Savior, that having been justified by His grace we should become heirs, according to the hope of eternal life (Titus 3:4-7).

How to witness to the Muslim

1. Share with him the dread of God's law.
2. Disclose to the Muslim how you have per-

sonally broken God's law and inform him how he has too. Use specific commandments.
3. Inform him that he needs an infinite atonement and a Savior to remove his sins.
4. After he admits his need, offer him the gospel: Jesus died for our sins, was buried, and rose again on the third day.
5. Call him to repent and trust in Christ.

Access to God

> The curtain in the temple was torn from top to bottom. We have the access to our Father that no one else can have. We come to God's throne spotless, redeemed. ... In Him, we have become the righteousness of God.[18]

> The Koran never declares that God is love.

The Koran says, "To those who believe *and* do deeds of righteousness hath Allah promised forgiveness and a great reward" (Sura 5:9). Ask the Muslim if he is doing enough good deeds to receive salvation on Judgment Day? Remind him that his repentance must be perfectly sincere for the Koran says, "O ye who believe! Turn unto Allah in *sincere* repentance!" (66:8). Only the man, who is sincere, may receive forgiveness. Without faith in Christ, how can one know one is sincere enough to be forgiven of God? The real solution is Jesus who paid for our sins on the cross, once for all. Thus, Christians are safe and filled with hope in Him and do not have to fret about doing enough good works to be accepted (Romans 4:5). Christians do good works for the sake of love and gratitude.

Greater love hath no man than this, that a man lay down his life for his friends (John 15:13).

A Dialogue with a Lebanese Muslim

Tom the Muslim: I'm from Lebanon.

Mike: Do you know anything about Christianity?

Tom: Ah, just that you think God is a... a... a....

Mike: Trinity?

Tom: Yes.

Mike: That's a big difference. Do you go to a Middle Eastern Mosque?

Tom: No. There aren't any here. I go to one that is run by Muslims from Pakistan.

Mike: Are you allowed to go to a Christian Church.

Tom: Oh no. That's against our religion.

Mike: Do you ever make mistakes against God, do you ever sin?

Tom: Everyone makes sins. But we believe God has mercy. We intend not to make mistakes, but one can't do that. Being a human being you have to make mistakes. Every day you make mistakes. We pray to Allah that he will forgive us.

Mike: On what basis does he forgive you?

Tom: Because Allah is like this, he is merciful.

Mike: Do you believe in justice?

Tom: Yes.

Mike: God is perfect, if I sin against Him how do I get forgiveness? You see, in Christianity, we believe that God is just and merciful.

Tom: So do we.

Mike: If God is just and merciful, He cannot just forgive arbitrarily, to just say you are forgiven without a just reason, you are forgiven just because you are forgiven, that's not true justice. Real justice and justification come from the only true infinite atonement in all the world's religions: Christ dying on the cross for our sins, taking God's justice on His back for us, so that He removes our sins. In Islam, Hinduism, Taoism and all the religions of the world, they do not have an answer for our mistakes and our sins: my mistakes, your mistakes, and everybody's mistakes. Their god is merciful, but he gives up justice, and his grace isn't based on anything, so it takes away his justice. I hope I didn't talk too fast because I'm sure English is your second language.

Tom: Yeah, we think when Allah forgives us; it's his right to do it. We do not have the authority to interfere with his right. Allah says that he has the right to forgive. You can say this is beyond our understanding, so I can't answer you.

Mike: But that would be against the true God's nature. You see we have a different God than you do. Your god is Allah, our God is not Allah. Our God is not unjust. Our God is just. So, Islamic people have to say, Allah just does it. What we would term as arbitrary; there is no justice behind it, it's whimsical.

Tom: We have the Koran.

Mike: You have no proof that the Koran is divine revelation. Muhammad

Tom: You have no proof for the Bible.

Mike: Oh, yes, we have over 300 prophecies on Christ. We have the argument from the impossibility of the contrary. We have the resurrection of Jesus.

Tom: We have prophecy on Muhammad: "A Comforter shall come."

Mike: Well, the Bible says that is the Holy Spirit and not Muhammad. You don't think that Muhammad brought much comfort to the Christians do you. Forced conversions and harsh taxes exacted upon them if they didn't convert? The sword and high taxes do not bring much comfort do they? Remember that Christ had a few hundred prophecies predicting Christ's life, much greater than the four or five that Muslims try to twist to fit Muhammad.

Mike: Now, remember that Allah is capricious. He is unjust. He is not our God. You have a different god, his nature changes.

Tom: This is Islam. That's the difference between the Bible and the Koran.

Mike: You have a different god.

Tom: No. I pray to Allah to forgive me of my sins.

Mike: On what grounds does he forgive you? This is the crux of the matter.

Tom: This is beyond our understanding. God didn't tell us about this.

Mike: Notice what you have to say. Out of all the world's religions, only Christianity doesn't say what you just said. Christianity is the only religion in the world that doesn't teach that God just forgives without justice.

Tom: Should I believe in Christianity?

Mike: Yes.

Tom: I can't believe God would send his Son to die on the cross.

Mike: You see, that's how justice is met. That is the only way to assert God's mercy and justice.

Tom: I can't believe it!

Mike: You base your eternal destiny on a god who changes his mind. A god who says I forgive you on no basis. Christianity alone says that God's justice and mercy is met on the cross. I strongly suggest that you repent.

Tom: We will meet at doomsday.

Mike: The day Christ will come back as the Bible and the Koran assert. Jesus comes back not Muhammad. Interesting, isn't it?

Islam Comes Up Short: Logic is Universally Required

Since Islam teaches that Allah can deceive and speak lies, Islam cannot be the foundation for fixed moral law, including the commandment for truth telling. Additionally, since Allah can change his mind, he fails to account for the invariable laws of logic.

Only Christian theism can ground the laws of thought; and this is of momentous importance, because these laws are in force everywhere. The laws of logic are independent and transcendent of any organism. These laws are immaterial, unalterable, and universal, since they transcend all organisms (even if a fly avoids being smacked by a fly-swatter). They are true whether you constate them or not. Since they exist, and are universal in application, unchanging, transcendent, and immaterial, the biblical God is true for He is the unchanging, immaterial, transcendent, and universal foundation and fount.

The laws of reason are not reducible to matter since if they were, they would not be laws—laws are not something that can be physically examined. Moreover, since the principles of logic are universal in nature they are not reducible to any particular physical object or objects. But if they are not reducible matter what are they? A little girl cannot place them in a basket. A farmer cannot pick them from his field. A man cannot swing a bat and hit them. The laws of thought are immaterial and universal.

The Christian rational paradigm can account for the principles of logic is readily demonstrable, the world religions fail. Christianity allows for abstract and universal laws. The Christian worldview teaches that more things exist than material objects. Thus, it makes sense for there to be abstractions and immaterial forms, norms, universals, and laws. Moreover, the universality of logic is possible because it is grounded on the character of God, who has universal power and reach. God is by nature logical. And this all-powerful, all knowing God orders all things in accordance with them.

God is a Self-contained Being: Aseity

> Some non-Christian systems (as the polytheistic religions and modern philosophical "personalisms") posit personal gods of one kind or another, but those gods are not absolute in the sense of being self-contained. Other non-Christian systems accept absolute realties of various kinds, but those absolutes are not personal. Only in the biblical teaching are absoluteness and personality combined in the Supreme being."[19]

> First and foremost among the attributes, we, therefore, mention the independence or self-existence of God. ... He is self-contained rationality.[20]

> All formations are impermanent and impersonal.[21]

Yahweh is a "self-individuated Spirit."[22] God is "self-contained fullness"[23] and "absolute personality."[24] Only Christian theism assents to a deity who is self-contained and personal. Considering that Islam teaches that their deity changes his mind and can lie, he lacks immutability, and thus is deficient of aseity. The biblical God has aseity. This means that God has self-existence, self-sufficiency, and He's not dependent or contingent upon anyone or anything. The power of His being is within Himself. "God is self-sufficient or self-contained in his being."[25] Nonexistence is impossible for God, yet the Muslim god is not absolutely needed or necessary forasmuch as he fails to account for immutables (Allah changes his mind) and universal moral law (Allah can lie). Allah is not a personal being or a thing; and is inscrutably arbitrary in his decrees. The Islamic god is fickle and capricious. This notion yields inconsistency and change; for Allah can do anything, including lie. He can deceive and mislead. He cannot ground changeless things for he is not bound to a nature. Changeless things, such as mathematics, logic, and moral law, exist and these require that which cannot change and cannot lie: the biblical God.

Considering that Allah can change his mind, he cannot be the ground for induction. Nobody has observed, or experienced the future, and no man knows what the relationship of the past is with the future. So, every time someone expects something to happen in the future based on the past experiences, he is assuming the Christian view of the universe, that God controls all things, and keeps them regular and predictable.

> The sovereign God is not someone who is beyond reach or beyond knowing.[26]

Van Til stressed the interlinking of God's attributes in that the "immutability of God is involved in his aseity." Since God is self-sufficient, He does not need to change like the Muslim deity can. There must be a foundation, somewhere, that is unchanging and has aseity. Van Til illuminates this: "We must rather reason that unless God exists as ultimate, as self-subsistent, we could not know anything, we could not even reason that God does not exist, nor could we even ask a question about God."[27] There must be a certain, absolute, self-sufficient, and unchanging basis for the intelligibility of our world: God. He must exist to account for the unchanging and transcendent laws of logic. Allah cannot supply the required pre-necessities for absolute and unchanging realities. Only the Lord God can. Even if Allah could account for the laws of logic, there is no basis for using such laws (since Allah is arbitrary) to understand and interpret the world. Such laws simply would not apply. The true God alone has the ability and character to provide that which is necessary to make sense out of reality.

Van Til remarked that "God is absolute. He is autonomous."[28] Man cannot be autonomous (not subject to the rule or authority of another) and the Muslim doctrine of Allah cannot be autonomous. For strict autonomy one must have true personality (Allah is not a person and lacks personality), aseity, self-rule, and supreme sovereignty which only the true God has.

The Christian God has no Shadow of Turning: Immutability

> Every good gift and every perfect gift is from above, and comes down from the Father of lights, with whom there is no variation or shadow of turning (James 1:17).

> For I am the LORD, I do not change (Malachi 3:6).
>
> There is no change in His being, His attributes, His purpose, His motives of action.29
>
> Immutability is one of the Divine perfections. ... It is one of the excellencies of the creature which distinguishes Him from all creatures. God is perceptually the same: subject to no changing His being, attributes, or determinations.30
>
> God is pure actuality–I am that I am–He has not potentiality. That which changes must possess the potential to change (Thomas Aquinas, *Summa Theologica* 1a. 9.1).

Thomas Aquinas noted, "That which is perfect cannot change." Allah can lie and change his decisions, thus he changes, he is not perfect, therefore he cannot be God; and Yahweh declares that false gods do not exist. Berkof further comments that "God never changes"31 and adds that "God's unchanging character sets Him apart from everything."32 All other claimed deities are deficient of full immutability. Yahweh alone is not mutable. Immutability is required for intelligibility, considering that the laws of reason do not change, and require an unchanging foundation, and web of necessities (moral law, mathematics, universals, etc.).

The only God that anyone can be certain exists is the God of the Bible. Van Til knew from Scripture that "the best and only possible proof for the existence of...God is that his existence is required for the uniformity of nature and the coherence of all things in the world."[33] For the Muslim deity and all the other declared gods cannot provide the necessary preconditions for the unity and coherence of all things including the laws of thought and the intelligibility of our experience. The laws of reason, communication, and rational arguments all rely on the laws of logic, as well as their application to the world of contingent experience, which God presides over as both Creator and Lord. The living God is required to account for the universal, transcendent, and immutable laws of logic. For the "existence of God is the presupposition of all possible predication."[34] A sovereign, unchangeable, and transcendent God must live to supply all the *a priori* conditions that are needed to communicate and understand our world. This is one of the reasons Bahnsen pressed that "only the Christian worldview can account for the objective validity and demands of logical consistency."[35] Only the biblical faith administers the prior rational essentials for logic and the reasonable comprehension of the creation and our encounters within our world.

One cannot truly know anything unless there is an unchanging foundation for knowledge. Bahnsen correctly asserted that "any knowledge that can really be called knowledge must be changeless, comprehensive knowledge."[36] Islam cannot offer that source, considering their god changes his decrees. Our changing universe cannot be the basis for knowledge, for it changes too. The Rock, the immutable God, enthroned as supreme, must be the foundation for knowledge. Without that changeless God, one has no unchanging reference point and ground for knowing what we know.

Christianity asserts that the laws of logic are invariant. If the laws of logic are not fixed, as allotheists claim, and they change in regions, then just ask the Muslim or Hindu (or atheist) to write one paragraph without using the Law of Non-contradiction. Encourage him to try this in any region at any time. If the Law of Non-contradiction does not change tonight for them, ask them to try again tomorrow, or even next year. They will soon discover that they cannot write one paragraph without the laws of logic. Yahweh is certain for He alone provides the necessary and immutable ground for the laws of logic.

An Arbitrary god cannot be the True God

Allah is described as "inscrutably arbitrary" in his decrees. Allah can do anything, including lying and changing his promises. Islamic theology postulates a fickle, capricious, untrustworthy being that is inconsistent, irregular, and has a mutable will. He can tell falsehoods and hoodwink men. This theology declares that this god can change for he is not bound to a nature, so he can lie and deceive. Yahweh is bound to his good moral nature. He cannot lie and He always keeps his promises.

Christian theism alone is true and rational:

- r V s.
- r = laws of logic are immutable.
- s = laws of logic are not immutable.

- Christians affirm r.
- Muslim philosophy affirms s.
- s is not sufficient to h (explain human experience).
- g (the Christian God) is necessary to h.
- h V –h.
- h is necessary.

- So h.
- g is necessary.
- So, the Christian God is necessary.

Yahweh is Love

God is love (1 John 4:9).

For God so loved the world that He gave His only begotten Son, that whoever believes in Him should not perish but have everlasting life (John 3:16).

It is not simply that God "loves," but that He is love itself. Love is...His very nature.37

The Islamic doctrine of God is centered on power and will. There is virtually no room for love.38

God's love is established on His nature. His nature does not change. Considering that God's love is bound to His character and being, His love is tied to His changelessness, sovereignty, and goodness. God declares His love for His covenant children, a love which will never change because God never changes. Likewise He, unlike Allah, cannot lie and deny His promises. The god of the Koran is never named as the God of love. Not once. He is not the ultimate source of eternal love. But the true God is the God of love and because He does not change and He is faithful, He will love those who are His forever and ever.

In contrast to the Islamic deity, Pink expounds an important aspect of God's nature for "God Himself is eternal, and God is love, therefore, as God Himself had no beginning, His love had none." God's love never is altered. Human love at times fails. We may not hold, hug, and care for a family member during a spell of annoyance or selfishness; one may even walk out on one's family. Some folks may have a little toddler come up and surprise them, and plant a big kiss on their cheek and they may push the little one away because people can change and experience moodiness. Allah changes and may have mood swings. And he is never declared the God of love. Letham adds that "God is the undivided Trinity, in which the three indwell each other in love."[39] The Lord of Scripture loves His children from everlasting to everlasting. He does not change.

- Love that rises upward is worship.
- Love that reaches outward is compassion.
- Love that condescends is grace.

The Only Solution for Sin: The Cross

> For the message of the cross is foolishness to those who are perishing, but to us who are being saved it is the power of God. For it is written: "I will destroy the wisdom of the wise, and bring to nothing the understanding of the prudent" (1 Corinthians 1:18-19).

Islam, like all other non-Christian religions, lacks an eternal atonement. God furnished this atonement through the cross of Jesus Christ. It is the power of the Lord of the universe unto salvation unto all who believe. Early church history tells us how the sign of the cross brought Cyprian to salvation. He was a warlock and he was going to rape a Christian girl. But when she made the sign of the cross he was decked, blasted, and knocked out cold. And he confessed that he had a revelation of Jesus. He became a Christian, and later a famous Christian bishop. Yet, we must always affirm that symbols, icons, and rituals do not save and cannot deliver effectual application of redemption, only the true cross does.

> And if by grace, then it is no longer of works; otherwise grace is no longer grace. But if it is of works, it is no longer grace; otherwise work is no longer work (Romans 11:6).

The Apostles' Creed professes, "I believe Jesus Christ suffered under Pontius Pilate, was crucified, dead, and buried." To receive the remission of sins, one must believe in the cross. Paul said, "God forbid that I glory in anything except the cross of Jesus Christ my Lord." Good works flow from our gift of salvation and when someone comes to the cross and receives Jesus Christ as Lord and Savior, then the good works flow from that. True salvation results in good works and a more godly life. But salvation is by the grace of God through faith alone because of Christ alone. This stupendous grace is only found in Christian theism. Islam cannot offer free grace and that is one of the reasons suicide bombers rush to blow up themselves and killed innocents: the escape of Allah's judgment and the hope of eternal joy in Paradise with seventy virgins. Thus we must preach Christ and Him crucified to the Muslim and the non-Muslim.

For what does the Scripture say? "Abraham believed God, and it was accounted to him for righteousness." Now to him who works, the wages are not counted as grace but as debt. But to him who does not work but believes on Him who justifies the ungodly, his faith is accounted for righteousness, just as David also describes the blessedness of the man to whom God imputes righteousness apart from works: "Blessed are those whose lawless deeds are forgiven, and whose sins are covered; blessed is the man to whom the LORD shall not impute sin" (Romans 4:3-8).

Without True Attributes: No Necessities for Intelligibility

You cannot supply what you do not have (Thomas Aquinas).

Allah is declared good, not because He is intrinsically morally good, but inasmuch as He causes good things to occur. Yahweh in contrast, is good and causes good. In Islam Allah is utterly unknowable, He does not reveal himself, but reveals only his will. Yahweh reveals both His will and Himself. Since Allah is neither good nor logical, for Allah lacks all attributes, he fails to provide the eternal and immutable ground for the laws of logic and moral law.

- Moral law and the laws of logic are necessary for intelligibility.
- To deny intelligibility requires intelligibility.
- There is intelligibility.
- Allah does not exist as God.

NOTES

1. Ravi Zacharias, *Light in the Shadow of Jihad*, (Multnomah, Sisters: OR, 2002), p. 100.
2. Darrell L. Bock, *Can I Trust the Bible?* (RZIM, Norcross: GA, 2001), p. 51.
3. Bernard Lewis, *Islam in History*, (Open Court, Peru: IL, 1993), p. 283.
4. Ibid., p. 364.
5. Hugh Goddard, *A History of Christian-Muslim Relations*, (New Amsterdam Publications, Chicago: IL, 2000), p. 62.
6. Frederick Buechner, *Wishful Thinking,* (Harper, San Francisco: CA, 1993), p. 21.
7. Ernest C. Reisinger, *The Law and the Gospel*, (P & R, Phillipsburg: NJ, 1970), pp. 70-71.
8. Robert Letham, *The Holy Trinity*, p. 10.
9. Ibid.
10. Goddard, p. 62.
11. John Frame, *No Other God: A Response to Open Theism,* (P & R, Phillipsburg: NJ, 2001), p. 16.
12. Van Til, *Survey of Christian Epistemology*, p. 216.
13. Letham, p. 442.
14. Van Til, *Survey*, p. 201
15. Colin Brown, *Philosophy and the Christian Faith,* (IVP, London: UK, 1968), p. 248.
16. John Frame, *The Doctrine of Knowledge of God*, p. 175.
17. Robert Stern, *Transcendental Arguments and Skepticism,* (Oxford Press, New York: NY, 2000), p. 220.
18. Keith Green, *Make My Life a Prayer*, (Harvest House, Eugene: OR, 2001), p. 141
19. Frame, *Cornelius Van Til*, p. 58.

20. Van Til, *An Introduction to Systematic Theology*, (P & R, Phillipsburg: NJ, 1974), p. 206.
21. Eric Cheetham, *Mainstream Buddhism*, (Tuttle, Rutland: VT, 1994), p. 141.
22. Ibid.,Van Til, *An Introduction to Systematic Theology*, p. 233.
23. Van Til, *Defense of the Faith*, p. 42.
24. Ibid., p. 42.
25. Van Til, *Christian Apologetics*, (P & R, Phillipsburg: NJ, 1976), p. 7.
26. K. Scott Oliphint, *The Battle Belongs to the Lord*, (P & R, Phillipsburg: NJ, 2003), p. 161
27. Van Til, *An Introduction to Systematic Theology*, p. 102.
28. Van Til, *Christian Apologetics*, p. 7.
29. Louis Berkof, *Systematic Theology*, (Eerdmans, Grand Rapids: MI, [1939], 1993), p. 59.
30. Arthur W. Pink, *The Attributes of God*, (Baker, Grand Rapids, MI, 1975), p. 37.
31. Berkof, p. 35.
32. Ibid.
33. Van Til, *Christian Apologetics*, p. 64.
34. Ibid., p. 13.
35. Bahnsen, *Van Til's Apologetic,* p. 236.
36. Ibid., p. 319.
37. Pink, p. 77.
38. Letham, p. 442.
39. Ibid., p. 421.

CHAPTER Three
Hinduism: The Religion Of Karma

Reincarnation is anti-theistic. Pantheism is the foundation god of reincarnation thought. Pantheism is impersonal and declares there is neither good nor evil.[1]

One's deeds have an inescapable effect on one's destiny in this life and the next. Endless cycles of birth and death are required for men (or their impersonal soul) in order to shed the effects of matter before they are reincarnated into the One of timeless perfection. It is a theology without grace; men's actions, over vast eons of time, heal their former metaphysical condition.[2]

Hinduism is one of the most ancient religions of man. Its sacred writings are called the Vedas. The doctrine of soul-transmigration is an important teaching in the Vedas:

upon death, living things are reborn into different organisms. After one dies, one's new earth-suit is a result of how good or evil you were in your past lives. Your past deeds dispense you on the correct spot on the karmic cycle through the law of karma. You could in your next life end up a snail, a germ, weed or a man.

The Philosophic Problems of Hinduism

> The Trinity is not a mere oneness or a mere threeness, but always three in one. So, the creation is unity in plurality, fact in law, law in fact.[3]

Eastern religions place great stress on the notion of *tat tvam asi*: thou art that. The implication of that phrase is that everything that an individual sees or experiences is you and is one. Thus this indirectly denies the laws of logic (A is A and not Non-A), yet must employ logic in that denial. Hindu dogma rejects the personal Triune God who is the only being with aseity. They posit a god who is dependent and is part of the cosmos. So Hinduism is anti-theistic: it denies the existing independent God of Christianity. The Trinity solves the problem of the one and many, and like all non-Christian worldviews, Hinduism fails to solve this all encompassing puzzle of the one and many.

The Puzzle of the One and the Many

The rational problem of the one and many has been a knotty dilemma since the classical Greeks. And from Hume to Russell, modern thinkers have been perplexed to explain whether unity has priority or does diversity. Men have pondered the question, "Why does unity contain diversity?" No one found a compelling answer for the basis of the unity of the diverse parts and the thing that brings all this together. Some say that unity has the greater priority (Hinduism) while others declare that the diversity has the greater priority (Mormonism). Opposing this notion is the unity and diversity that is structured in the material world and in the spiritual world.

A human being is one person (unity - the one), yet that person is made up of many parts: arms, legs, eyes, liver, heart (diversity - the many). Each part contains many cells that make up that one organ. Each specific cell contains many molecules; each individual molecule, many atoms. Living things are individual things that are made up of diverse parts.

This one book is composed of many chapters. Each chapter is made up of many paragraphs; each one paragraph is made up of many sentences; each sentence, many words; and each word is composed of many letters. The truth of the one and many is an unavoidable aspect of any book. This truth adjoins everything. The only coherent solution was pressed by Van Til. He proposed that the Trinity alone has the capacity to ground the unity and diversity in equal ultimacy. The one and many are co-ternimas, co-infinite, co-universal, co-eternal within the nature of God. God is Father, Son, and Holy Spirit (diversity) and is one God (unity). The equal and universal ultimacy of all things is grounded and proceeds from the Trinity. Where unity and particularity harmoniously and infinitely coalesce, associate, commune, and inter-adhere.

Monism, Oneness, and Illusion

If one rejects Christian theism, one must be bound to a radical diversity or a sharp and unbending unity. If everything is ultimately composed of non-relating particulars, there is no place for laws and perceptual norms. This is self-nullifying: one must use the laws of logic to assert that claim. In touching communication, this radical diversity cannot unify brute facts and words. This unity is required in person to person communication. The denial of the necessity of the laws of logic in communication is also self-rebutting for it requires communication.

> The doctrine of the incarnation asserts that God took on flesh. The doctrine of monism asserts that out of God flesh and matter appeared, and eventually they must return to (or into) God. Monism implies that God is somehow incomplete.[4]

> What moves, what falls, what stands, what breathes, what does not breath, what—many are its forms—this, growth together, becomes just One.[5]

> If...all is one absolute reality, Brahman, why should man search for *moksha*? Logically, this pantheistic monism has a terrible defect, because, if all things are part of Brahman, the escape from *samsara* would be utterly unnecessary and meaningless.[6]

> If all things are just an illusion, is that sentence just an illusion?

The idea that everything is one and all the diversity is an illusion is another option (Hinduism and Buddhism). To toss away all the particulars is to toss away the particular theory itself. It saws off the plank it is resting on. This monism cannot be true for it defeats itself. If one truly believed that all is one and diversity is a mere illusion, why do Hindu's and Buddhists look both ways before they cross the street? Why do they flee from a house on fire? Why do they swim away from sharks? If the monist gets hit by a bus (or burned up or eaten) and all that is left of him is a big stain, this helps him meet his goal of oneness with the world. Plus he should not fear pain, since the car, fire, and shark are just illusions. There are no particular things such as cars, fire, and sharks. Obviously this is nonsense. One would not live long if one attempted to live out monism, additionally it is rationally self-demolishing.

Pantheism

> The pantheistic view regards God as the omnipresent substance which all things consist, the irresistible current or force which flows through all movement and life. He is not a person who knows and loves us, for he has no existence except as he exists in things.[7]

> Filled with Brahman are the things we see,
> Filled with Brahman are things we see not,
> From out of Brahman flows all that is:
> From Brahman all—yet is still the same
> (Upanishads).

Hinduism asserts that the One is the true, ultimate, and final reality. The particulars in our experience are illusionary (*maya*) and false. The oneness of the real is all there really is. Yet, without a ground that places equal ultimacy on both the one and many, an individual cannot account for the particular moral laws, and the particular and distinct laws of logic that are unified as universal in necessity and application.

Hindu thought stresses the oneness (unity) over the many (diversity). The notion that all is one is called monism and attempts to remove the Creator and creation distinction. This is linked to pantheism: the idea that all is God. If this notion is played out it requires everything to be an illusion and to be enlightened one is fused into the oneness as you realize that everything else is a mirage. This is self-nullifying inasmuch as the dogma that everything is an illusion, would thus be an illusion, hence it is fallacious.

- Any rational person = r, must presuppose:

- w = The world is intelligible and is not an illusion.

- r knows w is necessary but only if it is logically possible that r believes that w cannot be true and false simultaneously.

- r must know w only if there is some proposition: l = logic (fixed, atemporal, perpetual, non-tangible, universal) such that r knows that l is true and w entails:

- r must presuppose w and l, r must know w and l only if there is some proposition y = Yahweh (who is fixed ontologically, universal in power and knowledge, atemporal, and non-tangible is necessary to ground the fixed, universal, atemporal, and non-tangible laws of logic).

The denial of these propositions must presuppose their truth: Yahweh must exist as God and the world cannot be an illusion.

It is interesting to note that most practicing Hindus are polytheistic and believe and worship many gods. This leads them to stress the many over the one. Why worship that which is only an illusion? Why even participate in this rational and spiritual chimera?

Hinduism teaches that evil is just an illusion. Atheism has the same problem since it lacks an absolute moral standard, evil is illusionary. Atheists press that the existence of evil disproves God. But evil exists and the atheist claims fall flat. Their claims bounce back and slap the atheist in the face because he cannot identify evil as evil under his atheistic presuppositions. To mark anything as evil one needs an invariant universal moral code and atheism lacks this as does Hinduism. Hinduism is utterly deficient in this because everything is just an illusion, including any moral law and even evil itself.

God is Surely Good

When the Christian observes evil events or things in the world, he can, and should, retain consistency with his presupposition about God's goodness by now inferring that

> God has a morally good reason for the evil that exists. ... And God is surely good, the Christian will profess, so any evil we find must be compatible with God's goodness.8
>
> Give up the illusion that you are an individual self (Ashtavakra Gita).
>
> He who is subject to this illusion suffers many sorrows. To take this unreal for the real is bondage (*Sankara: The Crest Jewel of Hindu Wisdom*).

The belief that everything is *maya*, illusionary, denies real evil because it is just one more aspect of the omni-illusion. In this perspective one cannot truly claim that rape, genocide, mass pollution, child abuse or any wicked acts are evil. This confutes itself because lying would not be evil and it would not really be anything, just an aspect of the illusion. One could then lie repetitively and assert the opposite of what the Hindu really states. Since there are no distinctions within Hinduism, then all suppositions are just as valid as their antithesis. This is alogical and necessitates Christian truth. Furthermore, one could ask the Hindu if removing Hinduism from the earth would be evil.

If all is illusion, then that would imply that men, bugs, logic, ethics, Hinduism, and reincarnation are just illusions and in fact do not exist.

- Hinduism posits that all is *maya* (illusionary).
- This illusion would include Hinduism.
- On Hinduism's ground, Hinduism is an illusion.

- Illusions are false.
- Hinduism is false.

Monism is Irrational

Truth is one, the sages call it by many names (Hindu Vedas).

Give up the idea of "me" and "mine." As long as there is consciousness of diversity and not of unity in the self, a man ignorantly thinks of himself as a separate being (Srimad Bhagavatam 11:4).

The One appears to be many (Mundaka Upanishad 1.1:9).

Those who disparage reason, ironically...use reason to do so. They offer arguments, "reasons," why reason is worthless.9

Many may think since Hinduism is just an irrational religion that it is not relevant in the modern world, but they are incorrect. The first Hindu prayer was delivered by a Hindu chaplain in the U.S. Senate on July 2007. In his prayer to the Hindu gods, minister Rajan Zed added passages from Rig Veda, Upanishads, and the Bhagavad-Gita. Hinduism is the third largest religion in the world and it is developing its own anti-rational apologists to defend it as a culture and a religion. India has become more strident in its application of its anti-conversion laws. In many parts of India in is illegal to convert from a Hindu to a different religion. Truth, love, and logic are the tools required to prevail against legalized prejudice.

Absolute Oneness Disallows the Laws of Logic

Stipulating, as Hinduism does, that "truth is one," breaks the logical Law of Identity (A is A) and the Law of Non-contradiction (A cannot be A and non-A in the same manner). This is self-impaling considering that this proclamation is required to employ the very laws of logic that it denies, within itself. If it is true, it is false; if it is false, it is false. This posture of Hindu thought is irrational and self-confuting.

- Hinduism asserts that all is one.
- This denies the Law of Identity and the Law of Non-contradiction.
- Yet the assertion that "all is one" uses the laws of logic in that denial.
- Ergo, Hinduism is self-defeating.

If a Hindu, a Newager or another anti-rationalist promulgates the notion that the laws of logic are an illusion or are not necessary, all you have to do is tell them that they actually stated the opposite of what they really said. This will frustrate the Hindu until he understands that the laws of logic are used in all assertions. If he denies this, his statements can be repeated back to him as the opposite. Hinduism adds to its irrationality, when it denies that there are true distinctions. If distinctions do not exist, then there is no distinction between:

> True and False.
> Right and Wrong.
> Good and Bad.
> Yes and No.
> A and Non-A.

Karma Perpetuates Evil

> The man who knows me as I am loses nothing, that is, whatever he does (karma), even though he should slay his mother or his father.10

Karma is a significant doctrine of Hindu thought. It is the notion that all beings, after they die, come back in life after life until they obtain righteous enlightenment. But if all is one, and all things mere illusions, there cannot be anything that is bad that gives one "bad" karma. And escaping the karmic cycle is not good; it too is just an illusion. Being a Hindu cannot be good, nor can having oneself immersed in the sewage of the Ganges River. If everything lacks distinctions, there is no distinction between an illusion and not an illusion. Personal enlightenment is not right and everything else is neither good nor bad. Kissing my wife is not any different than killing an infant. Burning down a rainforest is not bad nor is planting a hundred trees a good action. This is illogical, nonsensical, and self-stultifying.

Pantheism is Anti-theism

Pantheism posits the idea that God is everything; God is not distinct from the creation. Pantheism negates the personality of God and His otherness from the universe; so, pantheism should be considered anti-theistic. Hinduism is pantheistic. Considering that pantheism posits the doctrine that the universe and all that it contains is God, or a part of God, it leads to idolatry. It is idolatrous since one can worship the creation, or its components, if when all is said and done, these things are really a part of God. In opposition,

Christian theism acknowledges that, while the universe and all its contents have been created by God, the cosmos is not God, or a part of Him. If all that exists in the created universe were suddenly to cease existing, God would not disappear, nor would He be minified in any attribute or proclivity. He existed before creating and fashioning the cosmos, and He would therefore exist if it were somehow blotted out. If God was the universe, He would lack personality, and therefore could not be the ground for eternal love, the laws of logic, and fixed moral law. Personality, distinctions, and obligations cannot arise from that which has no personality.

- Hinduism lacks a ground for personality and posits that personality is an illusion.
- Men have personalities.
- Hinduism is fallacious.

Reincarnation: I Was Napoleon

> Will the dead return to this earth? No, says Solomon: "Never again will they have a part in anything that happens under the sun."[11]

Reincarnation is "the process of coming into flesh again. Implied is the notion that is there is something to us that is separate from the flesh, or body, that returns after death."[12] The transmigration of a soul has a similar connotation. It is defined as "the crossing of the soul from one body to another."[13] You could have been a cockroach or a sewer rat in a past life, or maybe you were one of the numerous Julius Caesars or Napoleons whom multitudes of reincarnationists insist that they were in a past life. Hindu sage Paramahansa

Yogananda revealed that Abraham Lincoln had once been a "yogi in the Himalayas." Steven Rosen admits that "reincarnation forgetfulness" is a problem for those who believe in the transmigration of the soul.14 The answer he supplies is that past life amnesia is part of the process of learning. This is a weak answer at best and contains its own seeds of destruction. When I teach my children, I point out that they should remember their past mistakes and learn from them in order that they can avoid making the same mistakes later. But reincarnation forgetfulness actually inhibits learning and growing as a human soul. Why does it take hypnosis, endless chanting, hypno-regression therapy or Wu Li Masters to bring back simple memories from a past lifetime? A lifetime lived with failures, flops, foibles, and mistakes nets nothing learned.

The notion of reincarnation is a major tenet of the Hindu religion. And according to a 2005 *Gallup Poll*, 20 percent of all American adults believe in reincarnation. *Newsweek* magazine, in August of 2007, reported that China banned Buddhist monks in Tibet from reincarnating without government approval. Many people and some absurd governments affirm this Eastern tenet. Hinduism adds that man really desires full liberation, called *mukti*, and emancipation from the limits of the illusionary flesh and material world. Obviously, Christ as Redeemer and Savior, is the key to the issue that Hinduism has identified: sin and failings. Jesus Christ has redeemed His people from sin, bondage, and iniquitous imprisonment. Hinduism wrestles with this problem, but it never really explains why the problem exists in the first place. In the Bible, we see that all of creation has been subjected to futility as a result of the fall of man.

The way in which the Hindu discovers enlightenment is to

be infused in a union with Brahman. Nevertheless, Jesus Christ supplied perfect and eternal reconciliation between Yahweh and believing sinful men, through the work of the cross. Additionally, the Holy Spirit brings true union with God and the believer. The mystical union with God through Christ by the Holy Spirit requires no work, merit or effort on the part of the Christian. Rather, God gave His only begotten Son as a free gift by free grace.

> That the God of our Lord Jesus Christ, the Father of glory, may give to you the spirit of wisdom and revelation in the knowledge of Him, the eyes of your understanding being enlightened; that you may know what is the hope of His calling, what are the riches of the glory of His inheritance in the saints, and what is the exceeding greatness of His power toward us who believe, according to the working of His mighty power (Ephesians 1:17-19).

A Conversation with a Hindu

> Hindu Tom: The laws of logic are not necessary.
>
> Christian Lance (affirming logic): So you agree that the laws of logic are necessary.
>
> Tom: No, I said that the laws of logic are not necessary.
>
> Lance: So, you agree that the laws of logic are necessary.

Tom: No. Are you hard of hearing? I said that the laws of logic are not necessary.

Lance: So you agree that the laws of logic are necessary.

Tom: Why are you contradicting me? I said clearly that the laws of logic are not necessary.

Lance: So, you acknowledge that the laws of logic are necessary because you are upset that I contradicted you. For this to be a contradiction, one must really believe in the laws of logic, including the Law of Noncontradiction. One cannot avoid contradiction if one attempts to deny the laws of logic. To prove this, all I have to do is say that you said the opposite of what you really said. Therefore Hinduism and all alogical religions are necessarily false.

Accepted by the God

I recall standing within a few feet of a man who was participating in a religious ceremony. About one hundred hooks were thrust into his body…two spears pierced his mouth, from one cheek through the other. Above his head he carried a huge contraption from which more sharp points entered his flesh…all this was done without shedding a drop of blood to add the 'supernatu-

> ral' touch. Why was he doing this? To fulfill a vow he had made to his god.15

Whereby all men sin and are unrighteous in their being and actions, the solution is not additional self-centered works, but faith in a redeeming Savior. Christ died for the ungodly and doing good works cannot remove past misdeeds. If I murder two men and then clothe the homeless by the thousands over the next twenty years, I still owe a debt as a murder. My good deeds did not erase my past transgressions. Likewise, good works in the name of a religion do not remove my past sins and misdeeds. I need an atonement that rinses away my sins permanently and eternally. No other religion furnishes a Savior for only Christ dies for all my sins. One does not need to swallow glass, or eat rat dung, or walk on one leg for five years to obtain forgiveness. He needs to trust in Jesus Christ, His death and resurrection.

The Cross: Justice and Grace Meet

> There is no one to plead our cause in the courts of karma. ... The really frightening thing about karma is not so much that it is neither empathetic nor merciful—which it is not–but that there is not even any evidence that it is intelligent.16

Flee from desire and intention (Bhagavad Gita 4:19).

False gods do not satisfy and false religions do not supply atoning satisfaction. God, because He is righteous and holy, requires a just accounting for all souls. The duty of the believer is to show the Hindu that he has broken God's holy law. All Hindu's have trampled upon the first three commandments. We must place the law upon their hearts. We should urge them to give up their idols and come to the only true and living God. The Decalogue is to be employed to send them to Christ. They must understand that their good works cannot pay the penalty for past sins or karma. Jesus Christ paid the price for all the sins of the ungodly. Future good works cannot erase past transgressions.

> Therefore, by the deeds of the law no flesh
> will be justified in His sight, for by the law
> is the knowledge of sin (Romans 3:20).

The law reveals the sin of all human beings. When one turns and believes the gospel, his sins are forgiven by God's good grace through the cross. When he turns and trusts in Christ, he is forgiven of all his sins. God's great grace credits him with the perfect righteousness of Jesus Christ. The believer is now in right standing with God; and at his death, he will enter heaven's glory because of Christ. Christians are not to shrink back in declaring God's holiness. We must declare the holiness of God until the allotheist flees to Christ. Then we are to place Christ, the righteous King before them as Savior and Lord.

The Attributes of the true God: Supremacy

> Yours, O LORD, is the greatness, the power
> and the glory, the victory and the majesty;
> for all that is in heaven and in earth is
> Yours; Yours is the kingdom, O LORD, and
> You are exalted as head over all. Both riches

> and honor come from You, and You reign over all. In Your hand is power and might; in Your hand it is to make great and to give strength to all (1 Chronicles 29:11-12).

The true God is the being in which "nothing greater can be conceived."17 The Hindu gods are not supreme because they are just one among millions of deities. If a Hindu sect posits that their god is the greatest god, whether it is: Brahma, Shiva or Krishna, remember this god does not have the attributes of the true god. Another problem arises because Hinduism claims that all is one, thus god is everything, and he is nothing in particular. Additionally, everything is a mere illusion and that would include the Hindu gods. In contrast, the Bible declares that God "can do everything," and that no purpose of His can be withheld from Him (Job 42:2). But the thoughts of Shiva or Brahma could be hindered by Vishnu or Krishna or by another god with his own inherent limitations. Accordingly, it is obvious that these gods are not the God of the Bible. It is self-evident that they do not even exist.

God is a Self-contained Being

> And God said to Moses, "I AM WHO I AM." And He said, "Thus you shall say to the children of Israel, 'I AM has sent me to you'" (Exodus 3:14).

> The God of revelation is necessary and self-contained. Chief and at the forefront of His being is God's "independence or self-

existence of God. ... He is self-contained rationality."[18]

For their rock is not like our Rock (Deuteronomy 32:40).

Polytheism is a result of empty feelings and not revelation because "men have felt a lack in the gods that are made with man's hand and according to men's imagination."[19]

Many deities are praised in the Rig-veda. ... Hindus have at least 330 million gods.[20]

The Hindu faith offers the option of bowing before millions of gods and goddesses. Some may even bow down low, chant, and prostrate themselves "before a pile of yak dung."[21]

Shiva, Krishna, and Brahma are not self-contained but are part of the universe and the grand illusion. But the Lord God has complete aseity. This means that God has self-existence, self-sufficiency, and He is not dependent or contingent upon anyone or anything. The Hindu gods could not be without the illusionary universe. The Lord has power of His own ontology within Himself. The true God is "self-sufficient or self-contained in his being."[22] Nonexistence is impossible for God, yet possible for all the deities among the innumerable Hindu gods. Not one of the Hindu gods is universally necessary within himself.

The Hindu gods are just a part of the ongoing flux and cosmic oneness, but the transcendence and immutability of

God of the Bible "is involved in his aseity."[23] Since God is self-sufficient, He does not need to change, as do the karma encased false gods. Yet, there must be a foundation, somewhere, that is unchanging and has aseity. Deny that God exists as "ultimate, as self-subsistent, we could not know anything; we could not even reason that God exists, nor could we even ask a question about God and we would lack a ground for knowledge."[24] Knowledge is necessary, for even suggesting that there is no knowledge is in fact a knowledge claim. Logic demands a certain, absolute, self-sufficient, and unchanging basis for the intelligibility of our world: God. He must exist to account for the unchanging and transcendent laws of logic. The laws of logic are universally required to make any assertion about religion or the cosmos. The gods of polytheism cannot supply the required pre-necessities for absolute and unchanging realities. Only the Lord God can. In fact, Hinduism does not even attempt to account for the laws of logic, since they deny that there are laws of logic while they are utilizing them in their pronouncements. The Lord God of Israel alone has the nature and capacity to furnish that which is necessary to make sense out of religion and the world.

The Triune God is Certain and Necessary

The God of the Bible certainly lives and He is necessary in all possible worlds. All possible worlds require the laws of logic and the laws of morality. Van Til pressed that "the best and only possible proof for the existence of...God is that his existence is required for the uniformity of nature and the coherence of all things in the world."[25] Every false god of polytheism fails to dispense the necessary preconditions for the unity and coherence of all things. Considering that Hindu polytheism asserts that the world is really one and the diversity is just cosmic smoke and mirrors it is a non-rational religion. The laws of reason and the intelligibility of our experience cannot be accounted for by Hindu thought. And it should not be sought after because reason would just slow your progress in becoming one with the universe. This is self-refuting for all communication and rational arguments that the Hindu asserts, all rely on the laws of logic. The living God is required to account for the universal, transcendent, and immutable laws of logic. For the "existence of God is the presupposition of all possible predication."[26] A sovereign, unchangeable, and transcendent God must live to supply all the rational preconditions that are necessary to communicate and understand our world, all of which the Hindu is stuck doing too. But "only the Christian worldview can account for the objective validity and demands of logical consistency."[27] Only the thrice holy God supplies the *a priori* prerequisites for logic and the intelligibility of the world in its unity and diversity.

The fickle and battling gods of Hindus cannot be the basis for knowledge, for they change and are not sovereign. The invariant God, supreme in power and glory, must be the foundation for knowledge. Deny the changeless Almighty God, and one stumbles into rational insufficiency, for man lacks an invariant foundation for epistemology and understanding what we know.

- b V c.
- b = laws of logic must be real.
- c = laws of logic are not real.

- Christian theists affirm b.
- Hindus affirm c.

- c is not sufficient to q (explain human experience).
- g (Yahweh) is sufficient to q.
- q V -q.
- q is necessary.
- So q.
- Hence g is necessary.
- Yahweh is necessary.

Infinitely: A Limitless God is not the Hindu god

> God has attributes of infinity, eternity, and immutability.[28]

The Hindu gods are just large drops within the ocean of the universe or are the big ocean that receives the other drops, thus they are not infinite because the universe is not infinite. But the Lord God is boundless in the "fullness of his being. God is limitless in his existence, and therefore in his attributes."[29] This is not so with the irrational and capricious gods of polytheism. Time had a start and the Hindu gods are tied to space and time, thus they are limited and cannot be the true God. Still, if one denies the infinite and omniscient God, one cannot know anything at all. However, that would be self-refuting, therefore one must know some things, and there must be epistemic certainty somewhere. And to have a proper and consistent epistemic environment and to know anything truly, one must wield the laws of logic, and that necessitates the Triune God. For as much as "the self-contained ontological Trinity we have the foundational concept of a Christian theory of being, of knowledge, and action. Christians are interested in showing to those who believe in no God or in a God, a beyond, some ultimate or absolute, that it is this God in whom they must believe lest all meaning should disappear."[30] If all was an illusion and all meaning vanished, then that utterance would lose its meaning, thus it would not be true. The Lord God must be: He alone delivers the necessary anterior conditions for epistemology and understanding.

A god, who absorbs all and becomes all, is a contingent god. A contingent being is "one with 'a genuine liability to perish' or with a 'built-in process of corruption.'"[31] In various ways, the Hindu gods do absolve into nothingness and into everything. These gods are bound to the illusionary cosmos, but the God of Christianity is atemporal for He transcends time. If God did not transcend time and space, He would increase in knowledge and in strength as He receives all things in the ocean of being. These are attributes of the Eastern deities, but not the true God. God must be all-knowing and all-powerful. The false gods are limited, and attached to space and time; the infinite and Almighty God is transcendent over time. Therefore, He can be the foundation for logic, knowledge, moral law, and the coherence of our world. The Lord God alone is eternal and infinite as a person and power. God in Trinity exists, and His nonexistence is impossible. The gods of polytheism are not required for universals and absolutes. They are expendable and ontologically immanent; therefore, they are false deities.

Holiness: a Lasting Characteristic of God

> The LORD is righteous in all His ways,
> Holy in all His works (Psalms 145:17).

The Lord God, of Abraham, Isaac, and Jacob, alone is holy and has holiness as an immutable aspect of His being. The Bible asks the rhetorical question: "Who is like You, O LORD, among the gods? Who is like You, glorious in holiness, fearful in praises, doing wonders?" (Exodus 15:11). And then the word of God announces the answer: "No one is holy like the LORD, for there is none besides You, nor is there any rock like our God" (1 Samuel 2:2). Hinduism teaches that sin is an illusion and thus its opposite, holiness, is an illusion as well. Within Hindu worldview, sin and holiness are not real. This implies that their gods could not have holiness in their nature and character. But as Pink notes the true God is "only absolutely holy."

The moral law is an eternal aspect of the Triune God's nature. Moral law must exist inasmuch as it is self-defeating to assert the converse. Deny moral law and one can contradict any true statement made because lying would not be morally wrong. God has "absolute internal moral purity."[32] And, unlike the changing morphing gods of polytheism, the living God "is independently, infinitely, immutably Holy."[33]

The Eastern Religionist's gods are not ultimately ontologically superior to men; and therefore, could never be an actual god. Since all is an illusion and all is really one, the Hindu deities are internally inconsistent. Van Til inoculates: "With the righteousness of God, we signify the internal self-consistency of the divine being."[34] The gods of polytheism are not invariantly holy and righteous. They could never be a god for they lack immutability and holiness; and are fallacious myths. The holy God pronounces that these gods do not exist (Isaiah 43-45).

God is All-powerful: Almighty

> Whatever the LORD pleases He does, in heaven and in earth, in the seas and in all deep places (Psalms 135:6).
>
> You can do everything, and that no purpose of Yours can be withheld from You (Job 42:2).
>
> God is omnipotent. He has the ability to do anything.[35]

All authority and "power belongs to God" (Psalms 62:11). He possesses the mastery and might to enact His will at His mere pleasure. "As God hath a will to resolve what He deems good, so has He the power to execute His will."[36] The gods from Hinduism are devoid of this power for they are stuck on a metaphysical track that has a destination that they must and will submit: to be dissolved into a final eschatological monism and cosmic oneness. In direct contrast, the Lord God "is clothed in omnipotence"[37] Pink added that "he, who cannot do what he will and perform, cannot be God."[38]

The Hindu gods cannot do as they desire for they will bump into the realm or authority of another god, they are limited in nature, authority, and in scope. And they cannot do what they wished, since they will always have a plethora of gods throughout the universe to thwart their will. All of the other gods may be able to veto anything the other gods may desire to do, seeing that they have no unity of authority. And a god, who is stationed, in one spot at a time, cannot account for the omnipresent laws of reason. Yahweh is not limited to a particular place. He is not contained within one locality like gods who are absent of omnipresence. These gods are always just somewhere, but the true God is everywhere as are the laws of logic which depend on Him.

Goodness

Polytheism promulgates gods that do not have moral standards and who cannot be holy for these notions are just rational mirages. But "the goodness of God endures continually" (Psalms 52:1). Whereas the false gods are not god by nature and even deny the notion of good, the living God is "good" and He does "good" (Psalms 119:68). If good and evil are not real, then Brahma, Shiva, and Vishnu are not good. Yet "God only is infinitely good. A boundless goodness that knows no limits, a goodness as infinite as his essence, not only good, but goodness itself, the supreme inconceivable goodness."[39]

The Triune God's goodness rules out the possibility that the gods of the Eastern religions exist. God is inescapably good and immutable in His goodness. The false gods are beings that could not be the source of goodness, since by essence they are not good. Additionally they deny the real existence of good. This logically leaves the gods in the pitch-black void of nonexistence. Frame avouches that "God cannot be God without his goodness, his eternity and his love. In other words, He is necessarily good, wise, eternal, and loving."[40] An absolute and changeless foundation for goodness must subsist or we would have no moral law. Moral absolutes must be or we could not make sense out of our world. Without moral law, communication would be impossible because meaningful communication presupposes telling the truth. Moral law is also necessary for one to know what is good and what is evil. Without it, murdering and torturing little children would not be any different than pulling a few weeds from your backyard. The false gods cannot provide the pre-necessities for moral law considering that they reject the notions of bad and good. Only the supreme God of biblical revelation, who has always been good and is the basis of all goodness, can dispense those pre-essentials for moral law and goodness.

Yahweh the Fount of Love

The word of God discloses numerous times that "God is love" and loves His people (1 John 4:9; Deuteronomy 7:7). Along with Hindu's inability to offer a fixed rationale for justice, logic, and personal uniformity, it is too impoverished to offer a foundation for love. Considering everything is an illusion, love cannot be real. So the most important attribute in the universe is just a facade, a chimera: all the love between men and women, parents and children, humanity to God, with Hinduism it is all a sham.

Good thing the Eastern religions are not true. One can come to Christ whereas: "God so loved the world that He gave His only begotten Son, that whoever believes in Him should not perish but have everlasting life" (John 3:16). People can truly love God and love others because: "It is not simply that God 'loves,' but that He is love itself. Love is...His very nature."[41] That doctrine is part of the good news that Christianity renders to children of God. God's love is established on His nature. His nature does not change and cannot bear "a falsehood."[42] Considering that God's love is an inner aspect of His character and being,

His love is tied to His immutable sovereignty and goodness. God declares His love for His covenant children and that will never change because God's nature and decrees are invariant. Correspondingly, He, unlike the false gods, cannot lie and deny His covenant pledges one day in eternity. The true God knows not another god for the idols of men do not exist.

Love as an Illusion?

Since everything in the world is a rational and empirical chicanery within Hinduism, love does not truly subsist anywhere and the gods do not love their children for eternity. Polytheism is not the ultimate source of love whereas the deities know that real love is just a shadowy falsehood. But God Almighty is the God of love. And He is immutable, and He is true to His covenant promises; thus, He will love those who are His for eternity.

In matching up to the Eastern deities, God's love never is modified or mutated. Human love at times weakens and falls short. Men and women at times may not want to embrace, cuddle, and consider a loved-one during a moment of vexation, pride or self-centeredness; some even leave their homes permanently. A sudden tight squeeze from a family member may catch one off guard and result in an uncaring reaction; the God of love would never do that. The Lord of Scripture loves His children from everlasting to everlasting and He is changeless.

> For I am persuaded that neither death nor life, nor angels nor principalities nor powers, nor things present nor things to come, nor

> height nor depth, nor any other created thing, shall be able to separate us from the love of God which is in Christ Jesus our Lord (Romans 8:38).
>
> **Grace, Pardon, and Justification**
>
> The premise is the faithful God. The means is Jesus Christ—the way, the truth, and the life (John 14:6). ... This is the life that no religion can offer; neither the Taoist temple nor the higher Manichaean ethic will give such...meaning. Only what Jesus Christ did overcomes death itself and ushers in true freedom, the freedom of forgiveness and of power over all evil.[43]

Hinduism teaches that one obtains salvation, the escaping the karmic wheel, by practicing good works and following vedaic morals. Still, the biblical revelation offers free grace. Grace is unmerited favor. No one is good enough to achieve salvation. All men sin and need a Savior. Only Jesus Christ and His death on the cross delivers an infinite atonement by grace alone seeing that this is the only way one can make it to a indefectible and sin-free heaven.

The Hindu is like all men. He needs to hear the bad news of the condemnation that hangs over his head because of his sin and failures. The threats of the law will remind him of this problem. The law must be preached before the nonbeliever will appreciate propitiation (Christ through the cross turned away God's wrath and judgment due all people). One must know why he is under the wrath of God that was turned away at the cross. All have sinned and broken God's law. That warrants the wrath of God abiding on the non-Christian. Jesus Christ is the only propitiation for the wrath and judgment of the thrice Holy God.

> The warrant of faith is nothing less than the mercy of God in Jesus Christ.44

The movie *Always* has a scene, where Richard Dreyfess and John Goodman are flying water planes to help put out a large forest fire. Suddenly, John Goodman's plane's engine catches fire and Dreyfess sees this and flies down to drop his water load on Goodman's plane to save his friend's life. As he dives down, he cannot pull up in time and went though the forest fire and his plane exploded. He gave up his life for his friend. He went through the fire to save another. And that is an aspect of what Jesus Christ did on the cross. He gave up his life and went through a horrific fire of judgment, wrath, and pain for all who come to Him.

Everyone Needs Amazing Grace

> We write our own ticket to glory and gloom.45

> Whom God set forth as a propitiation by His blood, through faith, to demonstrate His righteousness because in His forbearance God had passed over the sins that were previously committed (Romans 3:25).

> As far as the east is from the west, so far has He removed our transgressions from us (Psalms 103:12).

One Way to God

A man asked the former Hindu, Debrinda Das: "Why did you become a Christian?" He replied that he had observed a Christian man on his death bed. He told how he had watched his face, as he died; and as his life dimmed, he died in great calm and peace. He had never "observed a Hindu dying in this manner; on the contrary, those he observed died in agony and great despair." This was not the case with the follower of Christ he watched pass on. So he became a Christian because of the peace and hope that Christians have when they die.

> And if by grace, then it is no longer of works; otherwise, grace is no longer grace. But, if it is of works, it is no longer grace; otherwise, work is no longer work (Romans 11:6).

A story is told (it may not be historical) of a young lady, who failed in an assassination attempt of Queen Elizabeth I of England. When she was dragged before the Queen, she begged for mercy and asked the Queen for grace. The Queen coldly looked down at her and asked, "If I show you grace, what promise will you make to me for the future?" The woman looked up and replied, "Grace that has conditions isn't grace at all." The Queen clearly moved responded, "You are correct. I pardon you completely of my grace." The woman was freed and Queen Elizabeth never had a more faithful and devoted servant than that woman who had intended to take her life. That is an important factor in the manner in which God's grace works. We all were enemies of God, but by grace alone, one comes to the King. This gives one a complete pardon; and for the rest of one's life, one is to faithfully serve God. The Christian faith is the only faith that offers free grace, full pardon, and the Holy

Spirit to serve God out of gratitude.

> Therefore, the LORD will wait, that He may be gracious to you; and therefore He will be exalted, that He may have mercy on you. For the LORD is a God of justice; blessed are all those who wait for Him (Isaiah 30:18).

God's free grace is unconditional, unlimited, and unending. His grace through the cross of Christ makes a powerful difference in the life of the believer. All people sin, and until they come to Christ, they will have feelings of guilt and shame. Repentance and faith in Christ brings expiation, pardon, justification, and the removal of shame and guilt. This is life changing and eternal good news.

God, the High and Lofty One: Above All

> God is infinitely higher than the highest being of which man can form a concept.[46]

God transcends the world and He also comes to humanity in His immanency. The Lord God has "dominion incomprehensibly above any dominion of man; and, by all the shadows drawn from the authority of one man over another, we can have but weak glimmerings of the authority and dominion of God."[47] The Bible declares that the universe came into existence by the power of God in a specific act of creation *ex nihilo* at precise moment in time. Unlike Eastern thought, the Second Law of Thermodynamics and modern cosmology insist that the cosmos had a beginning. The physical world is not eternal and this does not leave room for the eternal pursuit of cosmic oneness. Living beings are not eternally spinning on the karmic wheel and the universe is neither infinite nor eternal. The Bible and scientific research refute those notions.

It is rationally and ethically indispensable that there is a transcendent God to fashion and form the world to be intelligible. This cannot be a god that is limited as the false deities are. The world has to be intelligible or communication would be impossible. Communication is mandatory which presupposes the biblical God, and negates the possibility of the gods of polytheism.

The Lord God: Infinite and Absolute

> Then Jesus said to them again, "Most assuredly, I say to you, I am the door of the sheep. All who ever came before Me are thieves and robbers, but the sheep did not hear them. I am the door. If anyone enters by Me, he will be saved, and will go in and out and find pasture" (John 10:7-9).

It is a pre-necessity that a ground looms over and beyond the world, who predates the finitude of the cosmos and is infinite in being. God unaccompanied has this attribute. Additionally "God is infinite, so are His attributes. His holiness is absolute. His sovereignty is complete. His righteousness is perfect. He is utterly unchangeable, totally faithful, and limitless in power. His knowledge is inexhaustible, and His presence boundless."[48]

A great scientist was on a train and he lost his ticket. He

was frantically looking for it, but was not able to locate it. The conductor tried to calm him down and told him not to worry and that he believes that he had purchased a ticket. "You're very kind," the absent-minded scientist replied, "but I must find it; otherwise, I won't know where to get off!" As one looks out to the world, no matter how brilliant one is, a person needs an epistemic place to start and eternal acceptance to finish. If one is without a sure ground for knowledge and an infinite atonement, no one, including the Hindu, can find the way to knowledge and salvation.

Hinduism promotes a caste system based on prejudice and discrimination, which produces enormous cultural deprivation and mistreatment of men, women, and children, as it focuses more care upon cows, rats, and insects. As a religion and a philosophy, Hinduism is a self-annihilating philosophy of life, as it proclaims that all men, beauty, ideas, laws, forms, norms, meaning, honor, dignity, justice, ethics, truth, and reality are illusions. It cuts a hole in the box it lays in, a box full of gross notions and gurus.

- Hinduism asserts that true distinctions do not exist.
- The laws of logic are distinct from all other things.
- Hindus necessarily employ the laws of logic.
- Hinduism is self-refuting.

NOTES

1. Norman Geisler and J. Amano Yutaka, *The Reincarnation Sensation*, (Tyndale, Wheaton: IL, 1986), p. 164.
2. Gary North, *None Dare Call It Witchcraft*, (Arlington House, New Rochelle: NY, 1977), p. 31.
3. John Frame, *Cornelius Van Til: An Analysis of His Thought*, (P & R, Phillipsburg: NJ, 1995), p. 135.
4. North, p. 63.
5. R.C. Zaehner, translation, *Hindu Scriptures*, (Dent & Sons, London: UK, 1966), p. 39.
6. Yong Kim, *Oriental Thought*, (Helix Books, Totowa: NJ, 1973), p. 12.
7. A.A. Hodge, *Evangelical Theology*, (Banner of Truth, Carisle: PA, [1890], 1976), p. 108.
8. Bahnsen, *Always Ready*, pp. 171-172.
9. Daniel Taylor, *The Myth of Certainty*, (Zondervan, Grand Rapids: MI, 1992), p. 69.
10. Zaehner, p. 173.
11. E. La Gard Smith, *Out on a Broken Limb*, (Harvest House, Eugene: OR, 1986), p. 138.
12. Steven Rosen, *The Reincarnation Controversy*, (Torchlight, Badger: CA, 1997), p. 6.
13. Ibid.
14. Ibid., pp. 13-14.
15. Ravi Zacharias, *Recapture the Wonder*, (Intergrity, Nashville: TN, 2005), p.p. 74-75.
16. Smith, p. 144.
17. Alvin Plantinga, *God and Other Minds*, (Cornell University Press, Ithaca: NY, [1967], 1990),
1. p. 24.
18. Van Til, *An Introduction to Systematic Theology*, p. 206.

19. Ibid., p. 108.
20. V.P. Kanitkar, *World Faiths: Hinduism*, (NTC, Chicago: IL, 1995), pp. 35 & 44.
21. Sam Storms, *Pleasures Evermore*, (NavPress, Colorado Springs: CO, 2000), p. 145.
22. Van Til, *Christian Apologetics*, p. 7.
23. Van Til, *An Introduction to Systematic Theology*, p. 206.
24. Ibid., p. 102.
25. Van Til, *Christian Apologetics*, p. 64.
26. Ibid., p. 13.
27. Bahnsen, *Van Til's Apologetic,* p. 236.
28. Jonathan Edwards, S. Hyun Lee, Editor, *The Works of Jonathan Edwards Vol. 21*, (Yale Press, New Haven: CT), p. 131.
29. Van Til, *An Introduction to Systematic Theology*, p. 211.
30. Van Til, *Christian Apologetics*, p. 13.
31. Alvin Plantinga, *God and Other Minds*, p. 24.
32. Van Til, *An Introduction to Systematic Theology*, p. 244.
33. Pink, p. 41.
34. Van Til, *An Introduction to Systematic Theology*, p. 245.
35. Berkof, p. 76.
36. Pink, p. 46.
37. Ibid., p. 51.
38. Ibid., p. 46.
39. Stephen Charnock, *The Existence and Attributes of God*, (Baker Books, Grand Rapids: MI, [1684], 2000), p. 211, Vol. II.
40. John M. Frame, *No Other God: A Response to Open Theism*, p. 52.
41. Pink, p. 77.

42. Frame, *No Other Gods: A Response to Open Theism*, p. 56.
43. Edgar, p. 130.
44. Ibid., p. 46.
45. Virginia Hanson, *Karma: The Universal Law of Harmony*, (Quest, Wheaton: IL, 1982), p. 33.
46. Van Til, *An Introduction to Systematic Theology*, p. 206.
47. Charnock, p. 363, Vol. II.
48. William MacDonald, *Alone In Majesty,* (Thomas Nelson, Nashville: TN, 1994), p. 178.

CHAPTER Four
Buddhism: The Religion Of Buddha

Take careful heed to yourselves, for you saw no form, when the LORD spoke to you at Horeb out of the midst of the fire, lest you act corruptly, and make for yourselves a carved image in the form of any figure: the likeness of male or female (Deuteronomy 4:15-16).

That the God of our Lord Jesus Christ, the Father of glory, may give to you the spirit of wisdom and revelation in the knowledge of Him, the eyes of your understanding being *enlightened* (Ephesians 1:18-19).

Buddhism is an offshoot of Hinduism; in fact, it arose as an ideology against Brahmanical Hinduism.[1]

> Buddha is a Sanskrit or Pali word, an honorific title that refers to a person, who is awakened or enlightened, who has reached a higher level of consciousness.2
>
> The Buddhist traditions differ from Christianity in both goals and methods.3

The Buddha was born in a wealthy family in India as Gautama Siddhartha. He was a son of a king and lived his early life as a prince. He was protected in a palace, as he enjoyed many earthly delights of royalty. One day, he ventured out into the countryside, and observed "Four Troubling Sights," which vexed him deeply. He saw a sick man, an elderly man, and a deceased man. Gautama was deeply troubled over these first-hand experiences of pain and death. Later, he came upon a poor beggar. This monkish beggar told Gautama that he was striving for enlightenment through self-denial. Gautama felt like this was the true path, and pronounced that he would seek enlightenment in the same manner: a manner in which he would expound and codify for his disciples after he labored many years ruminating on the meaning of suffering and unhappiness. At some point in this cosmic quest, he sat in a lotus position under a Bodhi tree and was determined not to leave until he discovered enlightenment. When he finally stood up, he announced that he was enlightened, and therefore was a Buddha. It would have helped him more if a Christian missionary came across him and preached the gospel to this seeker of enlightenment.

> For My own sake, for My own sake, I will do it; for how should My name be profaned?

And I will not give My glory to another. ... I am He, I am the First, I am also the Last (Isaiah 48:11-12).

Although Gautama Buddha did not concern himself with God, the Buddhist theology that developed after him had Buddha as the universe.[4]

The most important difference between Christianity and Buddhism is in the nature and attributes of the founders of each religion. Buddha claimed that he was a mere man and not a god; Jesus Christ declared that He was God the Son. Jesus announced that He was the great "I Am," Yahweh in the flesh. Buddha taught his followers not to focus on him, but to understand and ponder his teachings, which are called the Dharma. Some Buddhist sects later divinized the Buddha, going directly against his teachings.

Buddha's Buddhism is not overtly atheistic; it does not officially reject a personal God. It is mute about theism. It presses notions that teach a man-centered self-sufficiency that lacks a need of a god; thus, it is more agnostic or non-theistic, than atheistic. Still, the Buddhist aim is not to glorify God and receive personal blessings, but the liberation of the Buddhist from the weight of self. This is one of the many reasons why it is a self-centered religion. That is an interesting paradox in that the ego is really an illusion within Buddhist thought. That implies that one ought to selfishly deny selfishness from a self that does not truly exist. The outworking of that concept would mean the negation of:

- Personal identity.
- True love.

- Genuine communication.
- Real relationships (no mothers, fathers, siblings, friends, and grandparents).

The truth of no truth becomes, inevitably, truth.5

Many Buddhists admit that they affirm a philosophy of nothingness that brings soulish emancipation. But who is being liberated if one does not really exist? And everything that I am attempting to deny does not genuinely subsist? Correspondingly, the Buddhist enlightenment is an illusion built upon an illusion for an illusion.

- Everything is an illusion.
- Everything includes the Buddha himself.
- The Buddha is just an illusion.
- Thus, the Buddha offers nothing.

Human Autonomy is Impossible

Without Me, you can do nothing (Jesus, Gospel of John 15:5).

The chief principal of apostate man is his own autonomy.6

One must trust his own mind.7

Buddha systematized spiritual ennoblement in his teaching, which included The Four Noble Truths (FNT or NT hereafter). The First NT is that life is basically suffering (*dukkha*). This means that the soul is out of harmony and seeks after the wrong things, and thus perpetuates the suffering.

The Second NT is a result of desire. All men suffer because we lack that which we want and receive the trouble, which we do not desire. This desire to have and to possess things is the cause of our suffering. An important part of enlightenment is the understanding that suffering is just an illusion, like desire, and one escapes this desire through following the Dharma (the law of life, one's duty within cultural norms or the basic philosophical principals of one's life in the world).

More Noble Truths

The Third NT is to strive to remove desire, and affirm that everything that seems real—things we seek—are all just illusions.

- If all desire is error and increases suffering,
- Then the desire to rid myself of desire is an error and actually increases suffering.
- I should not desire to completely stifle desire.
- I should desire Christ.

> One must control one's own mind. ... and Remove all the impurities of worldly passion and egoism.8

The Fourth NT instructs one how to extinguish desire which, as asserted above, is self-impaling. On this crucial issue—the diagnosis of the human problem—Christianity and Buddhism are infinitely different. Buddha teaches that our desires need to be subdued and annihilated, but Jesus presses men to cultivate passionate desires to please God and follow after love. Buddha attempts to rid men of suffering by denying one's aspirations and in promulgating the notion that desires are part of the vast illusion of life. This reveals that the real need that Buddhists have is for the forgiveness of sins and acceptance by God. Only Jesus can provide this solution. The Buddhist is taught to resolve to follow Dharma with precision so one can find Nirvana. By contrast, the Christian, by grace, obtains salvation as a gift from God through the person and work of Christ.

- All men sin.
- Buddhism fails to offer an atonement for sin.
- Christianity supplies an eternal atonement through Christ.
- One should reject Buddha and accept Christ.

As is the case with all non-Christian religions, Buddhism lacks the epistemic environment to supply the *a priori* conditions for reason. It teaches an anti-reason paradigm, and beyond that, is essentially illogical. According to Buddhism, all human experience is a mere illusion; and the world is rightly comprehended by antirational understanding because the world and all human experience are not real. This illusion must be affirmed to gain enlightenment. One must reject logic, truth, and reality to advance towards Nirvana.

- One must employ reason to promote the Buddhist teaching of anti-reason.
- Anti-reason is self-contradictory.
- Buddhism rejects the laws of reason; thus, it is self-contradictory, as it employs reason to reject reason.

- That which is self-contradictory is false.
- Buddhism is false.

What is Nirvana?

Millions of people in the East have a deep reverence for Buddha. Although he refused worship, and rejected the notion that he was a god, many honor him and worship him as a god. But Buddha taught that when he died, he was gone and one should not worship or pray to him. His followers should strive to find, walk, and work for their own path to Nirvana. One must overcome selfish desires and goals and embrace an emptiness (you can also ask them what Nirvana is, many do not know. From there, ask them if everything is an illusion, is the word and meaning of Nirvana an illusion?).

The correct manner to obtain disimprisonment and emancipation, one's infusion into Nirvana, is to follow the Eightfold Path. The first part of the path is to gain right understanding. This occurs when one accepts the Four Noble Truths. The next stage is embrace the correct motive and aim of true enlightenment. The third step is to practice the right use of the tongue. One must discern and guard one's words, and avoid troubling communication. Without right speech, one is on the wrong path.

The next rung, the forth step, is right practice, right action. We must go beyond just understanding our behavior, and actually live a more virtuous life, as we put off murder, stealing, lying, impure sexual encounters, and drunkenness. The fifth precept is for one to obtain a right and good vocation. One must aim to have a livelihood that promotes health, happiness, and life.

Depend on Yourself

The sixth step is proper exertion of one's aim and strength. The goal should be to use one's strength in the cause of right, the pure, and wellness and the denial of wicked thoughts, words, and actions. The seventh step is the ruminating examination of one's heart, life, action, and aims. One must examine one's emotions, thoughts, and goals and insure that they line up with the first six steps. Without a fixed moral standard and the empowerment of the Holy Spirit, the Buddhist is left with his own autonomy, and devoid of a power source. He lacks a moral foundation to discern right thoughts and actions. Furthermore, he does not have the dynamic power from God that the Christian possesses.

The Eighth Step

The last precept and eighth step of Buddha's Eightfold Path is developing proper consideration, sedulousness, and meditation. The typical Eastern techniques must be employed, such as yoga and concentrated meditation. These steps are to assist one in finding escape and release from the suffering of this world and to have the soul dispensed into the ultimate Nirvana.

The problem with the world is sin and not the lack of recognition that everything is an illusion. All men sin and our greatest need is forgiveness from sin and acceptance by God. Buddhism misses the most important problem (sin) and cannot offer the only solution (a Savior: Christ Jesus). Selfishness, misdeeds, bad thoughts, and impurity are not just to be avoided, but one needs remission from these sins. Buddha cannot furnish the solution, Jesus is the solution.

A Sure Appointment

> And as it is appointed for men to die once, but after this the judgment (Hebrews 9:27).
>
> We are confident, yes, well pleased rather to be absent from the body and to be present with the Lord (2 Corinthians 5:8).
>
> No origination, no extinction;
> No permanence, no impermanence;
> No identity, no difference (Buddhist Couplet).

Another important difference between Buddhism and Christianity lies in Buddha's belief in reincarnation. Reincarnation is erroneous because the Bible teaches that men are physically born once, die once, and then face the judgment. Furthermore, reincarnation is false because not only can it not solve evil, but it perpetuates evil. If a man rapes ten women, he must be raped or receive the equivalent in his next lives. The perpetrators of those future crimes against his reincarnated soul, they will have to suffer the karmic retribution in a future life, and on and on. With reincarnation, the evil goes on endlessly. Again, the true answer is faith in Christ whose atoning sacrifice takes away the sins of the world.

> Reincarnation is a falsehood, which is not only shameful, but also hazardous (Tertullian).
>
> The next day, John saw Jesus coming toward him, and said, "Behold! The Lamb of God who takes away the sin of the world" (John 1:29).

No Primary Sources

Buddhism is loaded down with philosophical and theological problems. But it also has *a posteroiri* issues too. The fountainhead of the evidential difficulties of Buddhism is it lacks any first hand and primary sources on the life and teachings of Buddha. The documents that exist fail the historicity test because they are dated many hundreds of years after the Buddha died. Edward Conze notes, in contrasting the primary sources of the New Testament with the lack of ancient attestation of the Buddhist documents, that "Buddhists possess nothing that corresponds to the New Testament." In contrast, Christianity supplies first hand eyewitnesses with documents dated within ten to thirty years after the death and resurrection of Christ.

The Lack of Historicity

Buddhism lacks a historical basis and one would be hard pressed to find historical reasons not to impute the idea that the Buddha is just a myth and a man made legend. Thus Buddhism is erected on falsehoods and dissimulation promulgated in the authority of one that history cannot prove even existed.

> "Come now, and let us reason together," says the LORD (Isaiah 1:18).
>
> In Him (Christ) are hidden all the treasures of wisdom and knowledge (Colossians 2:3).
>
> Reason is necessary for argumentation and hence cannot be argued against.[9]

Buddhism is a man-centered myth in contrast with the historicity of Christianity. Buddhism is antirational and embraces non-reason and delights in illogical notions. But Christianity is built on revelation and logic through the great Logos: Jesus. God's ontology is the base of logic and God cannot be illogical. God calls His people to "come and reason together." Many people of all faiths may embrace irrationality, but that goes against the admonitions of the Lord. And a consequential aspect of this reasoning process is to come in faith to Christ for the remission of one's sins.

God's Holiness Displayed through His Word

The Christian must share the bad news with the Buddhist. Then offer the grace of God in the gospel, if God changes the sinner's heart through the gospel, the convert will flee God's judgments and hurl himself upon Christ and His eternal mercy. We are not to shrink back in declaring God's holiness and His law to the lost. We must declare the holiness of God until the Buddhist honors God's holiness and discovers his need of a Savior.

> I say to you that likewise, there will be more
> joy in heaven over one sinner, who repents
> than over ninety-nine just persons who need
> no repentance (Luke 15:7).

When one shares the love of God without preaching God's holiness and His law, it weakens the sinner's sense of sin; then the lost sinner is not interested in the wondrous truth of the cross and justification. The law and the gospel, these are the means God uses to save lost sinners through His Spirit. The Buddhists need to hear the bad news of the wrath of God, the judgment of righteousness, and the offer of God's great grace in the person and work of Jesus Christ. The unpleasant reality, the lost person's position before a righteous God, is the reason that they must cast themselves upon the mercy of God in Christ. We are to placard Christ to the Buddhist. Christ is the righteous King, whom all men have offended in every point of His holy law, and that same Christ the Savior died for our transgressions. Buddha did not and could not accomplish this for the sinner.

An Attribute which Buddha is Deficient: Supremacy

> For, with God, nothing will be impossible (Luke 1:37).
>
> Yours, O LORD, is the greatness, the power and the glory, the victory and the majesty...and You reign over all. (1 Chronicles 29:11-12).
>
> The absolute and universal supremacy of God is plainly and positively affirmed in many Scriptures.[10]
>
> The Buddhist tradition has been unanimous that a Creator-God...simply does not exist.[11]

The Buddha never claimed to be supreme and even if he had, as a finite human being, he is devoid of infinite power and sovereignty. The base and wellspring for epistemic necessities do not lie in Buddha. This disqualifies him (or any mere man) to be the necessary and sufficient source that provides epistemic rights. Therefore, the Buddhist fails to offer a means to posit a rational fixed reckoning for knowledge.

The Buddha was contained within spatial and temporal circumscriptions. One cannot be supreme if one is bound to a particular spot in the universe. It is also very obvious that Buddha cannot be preeminent while lacking universality and immutability. He is not the Almighty God who dwells in majestic glory and power.

Buddha's Inferiority and Insufficiency

> Yet, I am the LORD your God...and you shall know no God but Me; for there is no Savior besides Me (Hosea 13:4).

> First and foremost among the attributes, we therefore mention the independence or self-existence of God. ... He is self-contained rationality.[12]

> He is said to live in himself, because He receives neither being nor life from any other source in any way. Hence, the chief title of God, by which He is distinguished from all idols, is that He is the living God.[13]

> God has the source of his existence in Himself.[14]

> God is self-existent, that is, He has ground of His existence in Himself. God...exists by the necessity of His own being, therefore necessarily.[15]

Buddha, like all men, is deficient of aseity. Aseity denotes that God has self-existence, self-sufficiency, and He is not dependent or contingent upon anything. The power of His being is within Himself. "God is self-sufficient or self-contained in his being."[16] Nonexistence is impossible for God, yet possible for the Buddha and the Tao (the illusionary whole or the way). The Buddha is not absolutely needed or necessary.

> In the beginning was the Tao (Chinese translation of John 1:1).
>
> Jesus said to him, "I am the way, the truth, and the life. No one comes to the Father except through Me" (John 14:6).
>
> If God were not immutable, He would not be God.[17]
>
> The immutability of God is a necessary concomitant of His aseity. It is that perfection of God by which He is devoid of all change.[18]

And aseity requires immutability. Men change, they change every moment. Humans are mutable but God is changeless and the "immutability of God is involved in his aseity."[19] Since God is self-sufficient, He does not change as does the foundation of Buddhism. There must be a foundation that is changeless and contains aseity. Van Til discloses this: "We must rather reason that unless God exists as ultimate, as self-subsistent, we could not know anything, we could not even reason that God does not exist, nor could we even ask a question about God."[20] It is a rational imperative to have a certain, absolute, self-sufficient, and invariant basis for the intelligibility of human experience. Only God has the changeless and sufficient ontology to be the adequate epistemic rock. He must exist to account for the unchanging and transcendent laws of thought. The Buddha and his Tao deny laws and distinctions, therefore Buddhism cannot supply the required pre-necessities for absolute and unchanging realities, such as the laws of logic; only the Lord God can.

- Christianity alone accounts for the universal, invariant Law of Identity and Law of Non-contradiction, which are distinct from one another.
- Buddhism must utilize these distinct laws, as it denies distinctions.
- Buddhism presupposes Christianity.

Man is not the Creator

Buddhist scholar Ikeda muses that "the external world is solely a creation of the human consciousness."[21] Gathering that the world was not created by him, and since it is not subject to his exclusive control, and Buddha claims that the world is an illusion, there is no basis for accounting for such laws to understand and interpret the world. Such laws simply would not exist. This is self-defeating as these laws govern all one communicates and performs. The laws of reason must be exercised to deny them. The true God alone has the ability and character to provide that which is necessary to make sense out of actuality.

Anti-Triune religion is excluded from possibility because its ultimate philosophical foundation rests on personal infallibility, which humans cannot possess. Additionally, the presuppositions of anti-Triune philosophy rest on the Psychological Fallacy, seeing that certain presuppositions of argumentation reveal themselves to be absolutely necessary and universal. And the human fallibility of Buddha cannot supply the universals, absolutes, and universal entities. All arguments that attempt to deny Christian theism, presuppose Christian theism to make their argument possible. The attempt to refute Christianity presupposes the invariant, timeless, immaterial, universal, unremitting laws of logic by which the invariant, timeless, immaterial, universal, endless God supplies the necessary preconditions. All things material and immaterial presuppose God.

> Lord GOD! Behold, You have made the heavens and the earth by Your great power and outstretched arm. There is nothing too hard for You (Jeremiah 32:17).

Van Til rightly descried "God is absolute. He is autonomous."[22] Human beings, including the Buddha, cannot own unyielding autonomy. For strict autonomy one must possess aseity, self-rule, and sovereignty, which only the Yahweh has. Buddhism thinks much too highly of men and places too much hope in their ability to achieve righteousness. Van Til comments: "The natural man virtually attributes to himself that which true Christian theology attributes to the self-contained God."[23] Christians must speak the truth in love and tear off the masks of pride and self-sufficiency of practicing and nonobservant Buddhists. Christ summons us to share our faith with patience, dignity, veracity, and compassion.

God is Immutable: Buddha and the Tao Are Mutable

> For I am the LORD, I do not change (Malachi 3:6).
>
> Immutability is one of the Divine perfections. ... It is one of the excellencies of the Creator which distinguishes Him from all creatures. God is perceptually the same: subject to no changing His being, attributes or determinations.[24]
>
> God is pure actuality–I am that I am–he has not potentiality. That which changes must possess the potential to change. But God has not potentiality, He is the immutable I AM (Thomas Aquinas, *Summa Theologica* 1a. 9.1).

James stipulates that in God "there is no variation or shadow of turning" (James 1:17). The Buddha and the Tao change and vary. This implies that the rational infrastructure of Buddhism is neither complete nor perfect. In contrast, the Lord God cannot change in His character and decrees. A fixed epistemic and moral ground is necessary to build a view of the world that brings coherence and unity that are required for intelligibility.

The God of the Bible establishes a rational base for understanding and intellectual adhesion. This is an important aspect of the certain proof for God's existence. Van Til commented that "the best and only possible proof for the existence of...God is that his existence is required for the uniformity of nature and the coherence of all things in the world."[25] Eastern thought and Buddhism in particular cannot provide the necessary rational pre-essentials for the unity and coherence of all things including the laws of reason. Fellowship, communication, and rational arguments all depend on the Law of Non-contradiction and the Law of Identity, as well as their application to the world of provisory experience, which God ordains, directs, and sustains as Lord. The living God is required to account for the universal, immaterial, transcendent, and unchanging laws of logic. For the "existence of God is the presupposition of all possible predication."[26] A sovereign, unchangeable, and transcendent God must live to supply all the *a priori* conditions that are needed to disseminate information and to comprehend our world. Bahnsen opined that "only the Christian worldview can account for the objective validity and demands of logical consistency."[27] Christianity uniquely disburses the prior rational necessities for logic and the required intelligibility.

> Every good gift and every perfect gift is from above, and comes down from the Father of lights, with whom there is no variation or shadow of turning (James 1:17).

Trust the Changeless Rock

It only makes sense to put your full faith in a being that is changeless. That which changes will fail. Mutable men, including teachers who claim enlightenment, will be faithless at times. But Yahweh is always faithful. He is the Rock of unmoving hope and purpose. God's faithfulness is not contingent on the faithfulness of men. God is immutable and remains perceptually faithful. God is unchangeable and He never differs from age to age. Unlike religious sages, God does not grow or develop for He does not vary from past, present, and future in any way. God has never been less infinite or less righteous than He is today or in the far distant future. God is self-existent and self-sufficient: He is changeless in His character. All that Yahweh is, He has always been, and He will always be.

Whereas all humans change, sin, and fail, God never slips or fails. Men forget and stumble but there is always a solid unchanging place to turn: God. In Yahweh, no change is possible. One can come to God in faith and one does not have to guess whether God will be found in a favorable disposition. God is always open to the needs and cares of His people. He does not change. He does not keep banking hours, He never closes on holidays. He never changes His mind and He always keeps His covenants and promises. He is not capricious nor arbitrary for His love never fades. Blessings come from His eternal and unchanging hand. The hand of even the most enlightened teacher, guru or avatar is in constant flux. One cannot depend on that which always changes.

The Infinite God Supplies Epistemic Rights: A Man Cannot

> By the infinity of God is meant the boundless fullness of His being. God is limitless in His existence, and therefore in His attributes.[28]
>
> Eternity is a perceptual duration, which hath neither beginning nor end; time hath both.[29]

The *sine qua non* epistemological starting point is infinite and all-knowing. Without this foundation, the God of Christianity, one cannot know anything at all. However, that would be self-contravening; therefore, rational beings have true, but partial, knowledge. And to know anything, one must utilize the laws of logic, and that requires the Lord God. Van Til observed that with "the self-contained ontological Trinity we have the foundational concept of a Christian theory of being, of knowledge, and action. Christians are interested in showing to those who believe in no God or in a God, a beyond, some ultimate or absolute, that it is this God in whom they must believe, lest all meaning should disappear."30 If all meaning disappeared as an illusion, then that proposition would forfeit its own meaning; thus, it would be false. Therefore, justified infinite knowledge is necessary. God alone has this attribute; hence He is necessary for true knowledge.

A holy man, who develops and attains, is a contingent individual. A contingent, finite being is devoid of the essential qualities to provide meaning (universality, infinity, immutability). No dependent entity "would survive an infinite stretch of time."31 The Buddha could not reveal infinite and necessary truth as a man who was temporal and stuck within time. The Lord God of Christianity is atemporal. He transcends time. If God did not transcend time and space, He would increase in knowledge (like Buddha), and decrease in strength (Second Law of Thermodynamics). These are attributes of finite beings, but not God. God by definition and necessity must be all-knowing and all-powerful. As Buddhism's source of knowledge is limited to time and finitude; the infinite and sovereign God is transcendent over time. Therefore, He can be the bedrock for reason, knowledge, moral absolutes, and the coherence of our experience. Yahweh is matchless in His eternity and infinitude.

The Tao

> Tao ... It's in an ant. It's in a weed. It's in excrement and urine (Chuang Tzv).
>
> It is really impossible to give it a name, but I call it Tao. Without wishing to define it, it could be called "The Whole" (Tao Te Ching).
>
> Tao is indefinable original totality. Ideas create the appearance of separate things (Tao Te Ching).

The Buddhist notion of the Tao (The Way or The Whole) attempts to define everything as nothing. It is a confusing and illogical notion that becomes an excuse for the men who lack answers. Christ as the Logos delivers all the answers for life and eternity as the bedrock for logic, moral absolutes, and intelligibility. Christ furnishes a rational epistemic environment, but Buddhism provides an irrational system and epistemic illusions.

- The Triune God exists and His nonexistence is impossible.
- Buddha's future nonexistence is possible.
- Buddha is not necessary for the Law of Identity, moral law, men, and things.
- Buddha and the Tao are not required for any universals and absolutes.
- Buddha is expendable and therefore cannot be the necessary and sufficient source of knowledge.
- God is the necessary and sufficient source of knowledge.

- God denies the claims of Buddha and the Tao.
- Buddha and the Tao are false.

I, even I, am the LORD, and besides Me there is no Savior (Isaiah 43:11).

God is All-powerful: Almighty

God has spoken once, twice I have heard this: that power belongs to God (Psalms 62:11).

As God hath a will to resolve what He deems good, so has He the power to execute His will.[32]

Christian theologians, those who mined the rich treasures of the word of God, have taught that God "is clothed in omnipotence."[33] One Reformed scholar noted that "he, who cannot do what he will and perform, cannot be God."[34] Buddha, the Dali Lama, and ten thousand monks cannot do everything they wish. The forces of nature, the will of other men, and circumstances limit the best of the sages. But God's power is unlimited within His nature. He can do anything that is logical and moral, and no one can impede His will. No one is like the true and living God: "Who is like You, O LORD, among the gods? Who is like You, glorious in holiness, fearful in praises, doing wonders?" (Exodus 15:11). Buddhism offers only fallible men and idols, and is altogether destitute of the righteous and magnificent attributes of Almighty God. Job inscribes that God does "great things, and unsearchable, marvelous things without number" (Job 5:9). An infinite and almighty epistemic base is required, and only God meets that requirement.

- Buddhism fails to supply transcendental necessities.
- Without transcendental necessities, Buddhism cannot account for knowledge, or even the claim that everything is an illusion.
- There must be knowledge.
- Buddhism is false.

> To God our Savior, Who alone is wise, be glory and majesty, dominion and power, both now and forever. Amen (Jude 1:25).

The Foundation of Goodness

> The goodness of God endures forever (Psalms 52:1).

> God only is infinitely good. A boundless goodness that knows no limits, a goodness as infinite as his essence, not only good, but goodness itself, the supreme inconceivable goodness."[35]

> God is *summum bonum,* the highest good.[36]

> It is this notion of the goodness of God that forms the foundation of true Christian ethics. God must be man's *summum bonum*.[37]

Yahweh is inevitably, perceptually good by essence; and changeless in His goodness. The base and wellspring of

Buddhism could not be the source of goodness, since by natural attributes the Buddha was not good; and he once was selfish and unenlightened. This means that he could not be the sustaining derivation, the standard of goodness. Frame places this before us: "God cannot be God without his goodness, his eternity and his love. In other words, He is necessarily good."[38] A flawless and changeless footing for goodness is mandatory or we could not have a fixed moral law that distinguishes good from evil. Without moral law, conversing and learning would not be possible because real and effective communication presupposes the binding restriction of lying and the obligatory mandate of truth telling. Moral absolutes cannot be real if everything is an illusion, yet without it, murdering and torturing infants would not be any different than trimming some leaves from your Maple tree. Buddhism cannot provide the pre-obligations for moral law. The Buddha was devoid of perfection and had to strive to change. If one is perfect, then there is no need to change. Moral law cannot change. Only the incomparable God of the biblical revelation, whose nature has always been good and is the bedrock of all goodness, can administer those pre-necessities for moral absolutes and the standard of goodness. Moral law is required for intelligibility and communication. Buddhist thought fails to deliver the *a priori* conditions for moral law.

Love is Eternal for God is Eternal

God is love (1 John 4:9).

The LORD loves you... (Deuteronomy 7:7).

For God so loved the world that He gave His

> only begotten Son, that whoever believes in Him should not perish but have everlasting life (John 3:16).
>
> By this we know love, because He laid down His life for us. And we also ought to lay down our lives for the brethren (1 John 3:16).
>
> It is not simply that God "loves," but that He is love itself. Love is...His very nature.[39]

Legitimate and lasting love is predicated from and rests on the nature of the loving God. His nature is not in flux. Frame writes: "God's love is a sovereign love—not, in the final analysis, a vulnerable love."[40] Since God's love is an invariant attribute of His being, His love is fastened to His immutability, aseity, and perfectly good will. God bestows His love on His covenant children, and this eternal love will never change because God never changes. Eastern religions do not offer a God of perfect perceptual love. The true God is the God of love and whereas He is not mutable and He is always faithful, He will love those who are His eternally. This is wonderful news that motivates believers to follow Jesus and love others as God's love and law demand.

> God is no abstract deity. He is not withdrawn from our affairs..., detached, afar; rather, He acts in history to sustain our lives at each moment. He is as to us as our very lives.[41]

God loves and His love is manifest in His unremitting care for His people. Pink dispatches a consequential doctrine regarding God's unchanging being for "God Himself is eternal, and God is love, therefore, as God Himself had no beginning, His love had none." The Lord's love is never modified. The love of men and women is open to change and often is mutable. And human love, offered as an illusion, is all the Buddhist can offer. The Lord of Scripture loves His people forever, and He does not vary.

God's Grace

> For all have sinned and fall short of the glory of God (Romans 3:23).
>
> And of His fullness we have all received, and grace for grace (John 1:16).
>
> The Buddhist notion of salvation is essentially humanistic.[42]
>
> Divine grace is the Sovereign and saving favor of God exercised in the bestowment of blessings upon those who have no merit in them and for which no compensation is demanded from them."[43]

The Eastern religions teach that salvation (reaching Nirvana or escaping the wheel of karma) is attained by good works and self effort. By contrast, Christianity teaches that one can only receive salvation (God's acceptance and heaven forever) by grace alone. Buddha demands that men deny their selfish aims through rigid and demanding thoughts, words, and actions. The good Buddhist must also affirm the grand illusion so he can one day find enlightenment and be fused into nothingness, by contrast, Christ loves, saves, and cares for His own eternally. Colin Brown sums up the grace given for our acceptance by God with these words: "Justification involves being accepted (by God) in spite of ourselves."[44] The Christian is approved, favored, forgiven, and loved eternally in heaven's bliss by God through faith in Christ by God's grace alone.

Everyone needs grace, not uncaring karma. The means out of judgment is not good works and law keeping. If one was to strive to keep the law in exact perfection, one's future good works and obedience could not erase past misdeeds and sin. God is just and His justice demands perfection. No man but Christ ever lived a perfect life. And heaven is perfect and sin cannot enter therein. A person needs all his sins removed, and this is what Christ accomplished for the believer. Jesus, through His death and resurrection, as one trusts in Him, He rinses away all the sin and guilt. Then He replaces the believer's imperfect record with His perfect record. This is called the great exchange. Living perfect future lives cannot pay the price for past sins in past lives. If I break into a house and steal some goods, and I face a judge, I deserve to go to jail. At my trial, if I promise never to do wrong again, I still must pay the price. How much more do men owe, who sin against a holy and just God? Karma is not the escape; it is a trap, and keeps you perpetually on the wheel of sin, without even the aid of remembering past lives to prevent future mistakes and transgressions.

Absolute Absolution

The way of Buddha cannot disperse absolution. We all need complete forgiveness or one faces eternal condemnation. It may be astonishing to many, but Christ notified all who will listen that hell is real and it is eternal. He taught this more than any other person in Scripture. Buddhists and non-Buddhists must repent and trust Jesus Christ for full pardon. One who believes in the Christ, His death and resurrection, receives justification. All their sins are removed from their spiritual account and Christ's unflawed life-record is bestowed to their spiritual account. This is the one means in which men can enter an indefectible, spotless heaven with God for eternity.

> To the praise of the glory of His grace, by which He has made us accepted in the Beloved. In Him we have redemption through His blood, the forgiveness of sins, according to the riches of His grace which He made to abound toward us in all wisdom and prudence (Ephesians 1:6-8).

Salvation is established and rests on God's mercy and not one's merit. Acceptance by God is based on God's promise and not one's performance. Jesus the Messiah came in the flesh and died in our place to right all our wrong through expiation and justification. Christ died for our mistakes, our sins, our wrongs to remove all our guilt, and provide peace with God. The person, who turns and trusts in Jesus, is free from condemnation, guilt, and the fear of death. This is truly amazing grace that no other religion can proffer.

> That in the ages to come, He might show the exceeding riches of His grace in His kindness toward us in Christ Jesus. For by grace you have been saved through faith, and that

not of yourselves; it is the gift of God, not of works, lest anyone should boast (Ephesians 2:7-9).

God is Infinite; Buddha is Finite

God is infinitely higher than the highest being of which man can form a concept.[45]

The word of God notifies humanity that the material cosmos was birthed by God Almighty by the word of His power in just a micro-flash. Modern cosmology promulgates that the universe began in a moment. The material universe is neither infinite nor eternal. And anything that it produced would also be destitute of infinitude and eternality, including enlightened men. Buddha commanded, "Seek the truth." Jesus announced that He was the truth. To seek the truth is to seek God in Christ.

Presuppositionalist architect Van Til postulates: "God is self-determinately internally active. God is self-predicator. God is life himself."[46] Buddha and all his disciples are circumscribed by spatial reality, a mastery and dominion that transcends them. But "space cannot circumscribe God because space depends on God and God is infinite."[47] There is a transcendent God that presides over all, including Buddha, who makes the intelligibility of the world possible. This transcendent being cannot be enlightened and is not restricted by his past and by space as a finite man. The intelligibility of the world persists and real communication is possible because Yahweh subsists. Communication is necessary, which presupposes the Triune God, and negates the possibility that Buddhist thought is authentic and veracious.

Yahweh: Eternal, Independent, and Autarchic

> Just as God is infinite, so are His attributes. His holiness is absolute. His sovereignty is complete. His righteousness is perfect. He is utterly unchangeable, totally faithful, and limitless in power. His knowledge is inexhaustible, and His presence boundless.[48]
>
> We are starved for the glory of God, not self. No one goes to the Grand Canyon to increase self-esteem.[49]

God is not bound by anything outside His divine nature. He holds complete independence and acts with exhaustive sovereignty. Isaac Watts anthems that God controls all things "by order from thy throne." This cannot be said of the best of men, even those who boast of their enlightenment. God is eternal and infinite. He controls all things that are known and unknown. He is the basis of true epistemology, ethics, and a coherent view of the world.

- Everything is an illusion.
- Everything includes Buddhism.
- Buddhism is just an illusion.
- Thus, in rejecting Buddhism, I am rejecting nothing.
- Therefore, one should receive Christ, and receive every blessing.

Share the Grace You Have Received

> For by grace, you have been saved through

> faith, and that not of yourselves; it is the gift of God, not of works, lest anyone should boast (Ephesian 2:8-9).

> Work for your salvation with diligence (Buddha's last words).

Tibetan Buddhism cannot offer propitiation to eternally escape the judgment behind their Wheel of Existence. This is a circle, gripped by the fangs and claws of a hideous black monster: the Prince of Death. Inside this wheel is a rooster, serpent, and a pig: "representing passion, wrath, and ignorance." In this circle are "naked people being dragged down to rebirth."[50] So much for the fun of spinning the karmic wheel. Reincarnation is a troubling and confusing notion. Grace is free and comes from a loving God, who offers a saving Savior in Christ.

Obviously, Buddha did not die for his followers nor did he offer to give his eternal love to them. He did not declare that he would always be with them. Furthermore he did not teach that one's sins could be pardoned and expiated by faith in him. Jesus Christ furnishes all of this and more. In Buddhism, there is no "guarantee of Nirvana."[51] Jesus beckoned "Come to me all who labor and are heavy laden." Believers are to share this great mercy and love of the majestic Savior.

The Call of the Good Shepherd

> Most assuredly, I say to you, he who does not enter the sheepfold by the door, but climbs up some other way, the same is a

> thief and a robber. But He who enters by the door is the shepherd of the sheep. To Him the doorkeeper opens, and the sheep hear His voice; and He calls his own sheep by name and leads them out (John 10:1-3).

The non-Christian must turn and come to Christ, receive unceasing forgiveness and unending love. The Broadway play *Life with Father* had a scene where Vinnie tells his loved-one that he has a sure place in heaven, but that he is not so sure about himself, but if he is denied entrance that he would "manage to get in some way—even if I have to climb the fence." And that is an aspect of a works based religious system, self-effort, even in the face of condemnation. But no one can ascend into God's perfect heaven with sin, stain, and iniquity of any sort. Men need pardon, eternal forgiveness of all their sins. If not, one is not perfect, and one is placed outside the pristine and perfect heaven. Enlightened teachers cannot offer you a door, a gate or a ladder to heaven's joy. An imperfect and finite human being does not have the capacity to climb over the fence and land in heaven. Jesus Christ is the door and the only way to the Father. People must reject self-effort and cast themselves upon Christ and His everlasting forgiveness.

> Behold what manner of love the Father has bestowed on us, that we should be called children of God! Therefore the world does not know us, because it did not know Him. ... And you know that He was manifested to take away our sins, and in Him there is no sin (1 John 3:1-5).

There was a clock scene in the last hours of Queen Anne's

life. This clock scene was Anne dying, weak, and feeble in her infirmity. She is lying on her bed waiting for her impending death. All of a sudden, she springs up out of her bed and stands in front of a hefty clock. She just abides there, with her eyes fixed on the large time piece. The startled attendant asked her if she had seen anything unusual about the clock. The queen did not respond, but laid back on her bed and expired. The queen died, and everyone will die. Spiritually, we need a clock scene. We need to spring up and realize that death awaits us all, and without remission of sins, only doom follows. Look at your watch or the clock on your phone; and let that remind you that one day you will face death. You need a saving Redeemer and that is Christ Jesus. Call out to God, turn from your ways, and believe on the Lord Jesus, and be saved.

> There is a notion abroad to win a man you must agree with him. Actually, the opposite is true. ... The man, who is going in the wrong direction, will never be set right by the affable religionist, who falls into step beside him and goes the same way. Someone must place himself across the path and insist that the straying man turn around and go in the right direction (G.K. Chesterton).

A parable is told about a Chinese man who desired to learn more about Christianity. He wanted to learn how it was different than Confucianism and Buddhism. A Christian told him, "If you fell into a pit and climbed out yourself, Confucius could come and instruct you to learn your lesson and avoid what made you fall into the hole. Buddha could walk by the pit and offer a hand to help you get out of the ditch. But Jesus would climb down into the pit and carry you out." Only Christ comes and rescues those who call upon His name. No other religious tradition offers salvation and hope by all-forgiving grace.

> Let it be known to you all, and to all the people of Israel, that by the name of Jesus Christ of Nazareth. ... There is no other name under heaven given among men by which we must be saved (Acts 4:10-12).

NOTES

1. Madasamy Thirumalai, *Sharing Your Faith with a Buddhist*, (Bethany House, Bloomington: MN, 2003), p. 16.
2. Ibid., p. 17.
3. Gerald McDermott, *Can an Evangelical Learn Anything from World Religions?* (IVP, Downers: IL, 2000), p. 214.
4. Thirumalai, p. 184.
5. David Bently Hart, *The Beauty of the Infinite*, (Eerdmans, Grand Rapids: MI, 2003), p. 7.
6. Gary North, p. 20.
7. Bukkyo Kyokai, *The Teachings of Buddha*, (Kosaido, Tokyo: Japan, 1966), p. 120.
8. Ibid., pp. 11 & 80.
9. Owen Anderson, *B.B. Warfield and Right Reason*, (University Press, New York: NY, 2006), p. 60.
10. Pink, p. 28.
11. *Sutras: Teachings of Buddha and Authorized Disciples*, p. 189.
12. Van Til, *An Introduction to Systematic Theology*, p. 206.
13. William Ames, *The Marrow of Theology,* (Baker Books, Grand Rapids: Michigan, 1997), p. 86.
14. Herman Bavinck, trans. William Hendriksen, *The Doctrine of God*, (Banner of Truth, Carisle: PA, 1977), p. 145.
15. Berkof, p. 58.
16. Van Til, *Christian Apologetics*, p. 7.
17. Bavinck, p. 147.
18. Berkof, p. 58.
19. Van Til, *An Introduction to Systematic Theology*, p. 206.

20. Ibid., p. 102.
21. Daisaku Ikeda, trans. Burton Watson, *Buddhism and the First Millenium*, (Kodansha, New York: NY, 1977), p. 151.
22. Van Til, *Christian Apologetics*, p. 7.
23. Ibid., p. 97.
24. Pink, p. 37.
25. Van Til, *Christian Apologetics*, p. 64.
26. Ibid., p. 13.
27. Bahnsen, *Van Til's Apologetic*, p. 236.
28. Van Til, *An Introduction to Systematic Theology*, p. 211.
29. Charnock, p. 279, Vol. I.
30. Van Til, *Christian Apologetics*, p. 13.
31. Alvin Plantinga, *God and Other Minds*, p. 24.
32. Pink, p. 46.
33. Ibid., p. 51.
34. Ibid., p. 46.
35. Charnock, p. 211, Vol. II.
36. Pink, p. 57.
37. Van Til, *An Introduction to Systematic Theology*, p. 238.
38. John M. Frame, *No Other God: A Response to Open Theism*, p. 52.
39. Pink, p. 77.
40. Frame, *No Other Gods: A Response to Open Theism*, p. 56.
41. Oliphint, p. 161.
42. Yong Kim, p. 45.
43. Pink, p. 66.
44. Colin Brown, p. 196.
45. Van Til, *An Introduction to Systematic Theology*, p. 206.
46. Ibid., p. 212.

47. Ibid., p. 215.
48. MacDonald, p. 178.
49. John Piper, *Seeing and Savoring Jesus Christ*, (Crossway, Wheaton: IL, 2001), p. 20.
50. Geoffrey Perringer, *The Faiths of Mankind*, (Crowell, New York: NY, 1964), p. 108.
51. Thirumalai, p. 155.

CHAPTER Five
Increasing Discernment

> Every word of God is pure: He is a shield unto them that put their trust in him. Add thou not unto his words, lest He reprove thee, and thou be found a liar (Proverbs 30:5-6).
>
> Whosoever despises the word shall be destroyed: but he that fears the commandment shall be rewarded (Proverbs 13:13).
>
> The grass withers, the flower fades: but the word of our God shall stand for ever (Isaiah 40:8).

The word of God is the most important discernment tool that God has given humanity. The Bible is necessary to make proper distinctions and to possess a logical and coherent worldview.

Developing Religious Discernment

> Jesus had appeared to his disciples three days after his crucifixion and that he was alive (Antiquities of the Jews).

If you came upon a fork in the road and you did not know which direction to take to reach your proper destination, and two men were there, but one was dead and one was alive, who would you ask directions? You could only ask the living man. And only Jesus Christ ever came back from the dead. He is alive and it is not possible to receive directions from the dead religious leaders.

The word of God declares that Jesus was raised from the dead. It is not possible for the resurrection of Christ to be false. One does not need history to verify that Christ is alive, yet in ancient history, all the sources that document the events surrounding the resurrection of Christ, record the fact of the empty tomb of the Lord. This includes non-Christian sources. First century Jewish historian Josephus noted Christ's death and the published the report of the resurrection of Jesus. The text in Josephus is so clear and so striking, and in exact line with the Gospels, that some skeptics question its authenticity.

Josephus on Christ

> About this time there lived Jesus, a wise man, if indeed it is lawful to call him a man, for he was a performer of wonderful deeds, a teacher of such men as are happy to accept the truth. He won over many of the Jews and

many of the Gentiles. He was the Christ, and when Pilate, at the suggestion of the leading men among us, had condemned him to the cross, those who had loved him at the first did not forsake him; for he appeared to them alive again on the third day, as the prophets of God had foretold these and ten thousand other wonders about him. And the tribe of Christians, so named from him, are not extinct to this day.

The paragraph in the work of Josephus, which documents the resurrection, is found in numerous assorted and diverse languages: Greek, Latin, Syriac, and Arabic, to posit just a handful. All of these texts, scattered throughout the world and held by groups that disagreed on issues, contain the assertion that Christ was seen alive.

This material of Josephus is dispersed broadly and translated in far too numerous dialects to be a corruption in the text. If one desired to change the text of Josephus, and add the resurrection assertion, he would have to travel on horse back around the known world and seize all the various texts of Josephus from opposing religious parties; then change every copy in all the various languages. So Josephus in the first century registers the fact of the resurrection of Christ. One can add Tacitus who noted the same historical facts. He imputed many of the same details about Christ in the late first and early second century. Lucian and Bar Serapion wrote of the same events in the second century. Clement in 95 A.D. annunciated that the disciples had been "fully assured by the resurrection of our Lord" (1 Clement 42:3-4).

The evidence that Christ rose from the dead:

- Friendly and hostile witnesses claim that Jesus was risen from the grave and that Christ appeared to His disciples and others, including over 500 people at one time.

- Every ancient historical source, friends and foes alike, document that the tomb of Christ was empty.

- The resurrection must be true inasmuch as without the word of God, which includes the resurrection, intelligibility is epistemologically lost. But there is and must be intelligibly, thus Christ is alive.

- Every piece of evidence requires the employment of the laws of logic and only Yahweh has the ontological stature to supply the preconditions for these laws. Hence, any discussion of evidence requires the God of the Bible.

There is something compelling about the way the Bible can both give a satisfying picture of the world and draw us to God's grace.[1]

Gaining Religious Discernment

How to acquire and gain religious discernment and avoid being deceived into a false religion:

1. Affirm a proper view of God (Exodus 20; John 14:6).

2. Worship God weekly with fellow Christians (Acts Chapters 2-4; Deuteronomy 5).

3. Affirm the inerrancy and sufficiency of Scripture; and study it as a disciple of Christ (2 Timothy 2:15 and 3:16-17; Hebrews 4:12).

4. Pray for wisdom and discernment (Proverbs 2:3-6; 1 Kings 3:5-10; James 1:5; Ephesians 1:17-19).

5. Obey God's word from a heart of love and gratitude (Titus 2:11-12; James 1:22).

6. Join and support a biblical church that practices discipline, liberty, godliness, and accountability (Acts 5).

7. Keep your eyes on Jesus (Hebrews 12:1-2; John 15)

    It is in Christ's love that we may have a clear idea of the glory of God.[2]

NOTES

1. Edgar, pp. 88-89.
2. John Owen, *The Glory of Christ*, (Banner of Truth, Carlisle: PA, reprint 2000), p. 17.

ALSO BY Michael A. Robinson

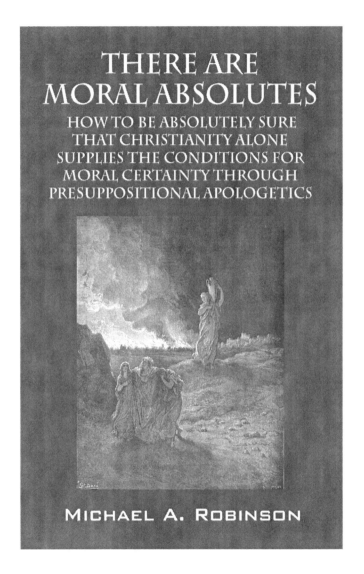

There Are Moral Absolutes

THERE ARE MORAL ABSOLUTES! How to Be Absolutely Sure That Christianity Alone Supplies The Conditions For Moral Certainty Through Presuppositional Apologetics Pastor Michael Allen Robinson,
    Today, many people assert that there are no moral absolutes. Yet arguing against unchanging moral truths is self-refuting. When one declares that there are no absolute moral laws, he assumes and desires that you take his statement as "true." The word "true" presupposes that there is a true and false, and a right and wrong. What the anti-moralist asserts defeats itself on its own grounds. If he objects to you pointing this out, he also refutes himself. To state that he objects to anything is to assume moral absolutes. Hence, his objection is false and self-nullifying. You ask him, "Do you think that it is 'wrong' to affirm absolutes?" If he answers "No," at that point he has contradicted himself and affirms moral absolutes. If he answers "Yes," you point out that this objection is an absolute moral truth, thus, he refutes himself and assumes the Christian worldview of absolute moral truths.

Learn more at:
www.outskirtspress.com/moralabsolutes

ALSO BY Michael A. Robinson

Presuppositional Apologetics

Greg L. Bahnsen befittingly argued: The Christian cannot forever be defensively constructing atomistic answers to the endless variety of unbelieving criticisms; he must take the offensive and show the unbeliever that he has no intelligible place to stand, no consistent epistemology, no justification for meaningful discourse, predication, or argumentation. The issue isn't just about evidence for the Bible and the Trinity. The certain proof for the Bible is that without God, one cannot account for evidence because God is the precondition for the laws of logic and the intelligibility of human experience. Logic that must be utilized in marshaling and pondering the evidence. Mormonism fails to supply the necessary prior conditions for logic. Only Christianity supplies the necessary preconditions for the transcendent, absolute, unchanging, universal, and immaterial laws of logic. A changing, material-only god cannot provide the needed a priori conditions for the laws of logic. Logic requires a transcendent, absolute, unchanging, and nonmaterial God. This is the certain argument. This argument grows in power when one attacks it. The argument grows in force because the rival must use logic to make an intellectual challenge. Logic requires God. Logic has no physical content. The abstract application of reason has no material content. Logic is essential and a precondition for any intelligent communication, but it was not invented by philosophers. Logic is the foundational instrument necessary for all discourse, debate, and science. Without using logic, one cannot even deny that logic is mandatory for communication. The precondition for the laws of logic is God. Without the sovereign, non-physical, transcendent, immutable, and universal God, one cannot justify transcendent, non-physical, universal, and abstract logic. Logic is absolutely necessary for the intelligibility of life and God is absolutely necessary for logic. Van Til comments: The natural man virtually attributes to himself that which true Christian theology attributes to the self-contained God.

Learn more at:
www.outskirtspress.com/PresuppositionalApologetics

ALSO BY Michael A. Robinson

Letter to an Atheist Nation

Presuppositional Apologetics Responds To: Letter to a Christian Nation

Michael Allen Robinson

Letter to an Atheist Nation

ATHEISM PROVES THEISM. You will apprehend and embrace Van Til and Bahnsen's Transcendental argument and: Disprove Atheism and Agnosticism, Demonstrate that God must exist, Rationally defeat Sam Harris' Anti-theistic Philosophy, Discover how reason and morality presuppose God, and Press presuppositional Apologetics to confound the Brights.

Michael Allen Robinson, a Reformed pastor and teacher at Christ Covenant Bible School, Las Vegas, Nevada, has equipped numerous Christians in utilizing presuppositional apologetics. He is available for speaking and teaching seminars. 800-647-9030. Puritan Presuppositional Press Las Vegas, Nevada.

Learn more at:
www.outskirtspress.com/lettertoanatheistnation

Printed in the United States
122060LV00002B/86/P